PIANO . VOCAL . GUITAR

P9-BYH-343

the music

glee

season two   volume 4

ISBN 978-1-61780-581-3

HAL•LEONARD®
CORPORATION
7777 W. BLUEMOUND RD. P.O. BOX 13819 MILWAUKEE, WI 53213

Visit Hal Leonard Online at
www.halleonard.com

EMPIRE STATE OF MIND

Words and Music by ALICIA KEYS, SHAWN CARTER,
JANE'T SEWELL, ANGELA HUNTE, AL SHUCKBURGH,
BERT KEYES and SYLVIA ROBINSON

Moderate Hip-Hop

Lyrics under the staves:

1. Yeah, yeah, I'm up at Brook-lyn, now I'm down in Tri-bec-a, right next to De Ni-ro, but I'll be hood for-ev-er. I'm the new Si-

2., 3. *(See Rap lyrics)*

* *Recorded a half step higher.*

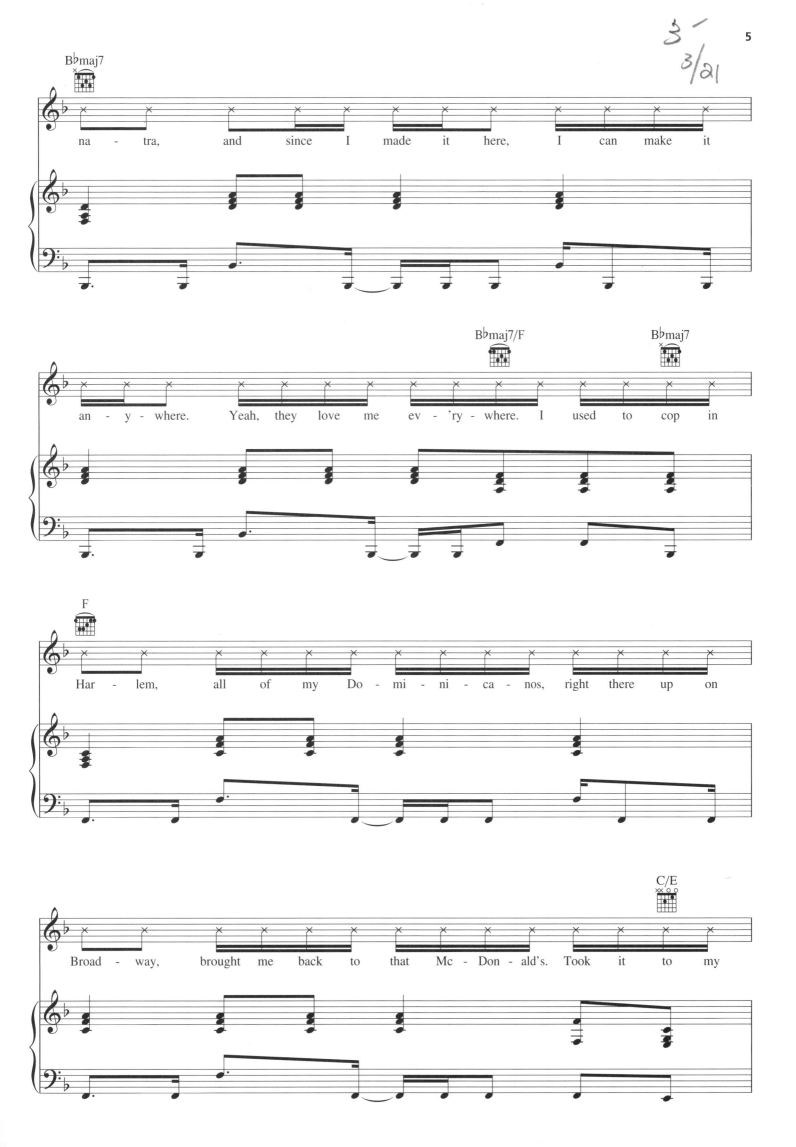

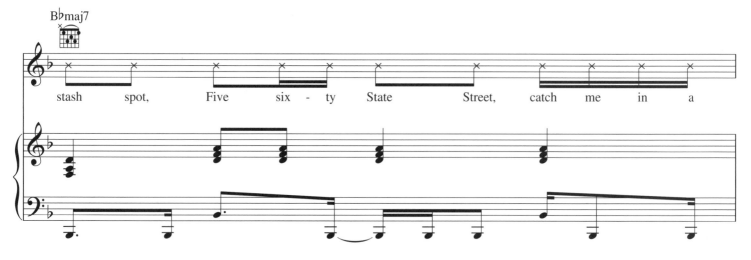

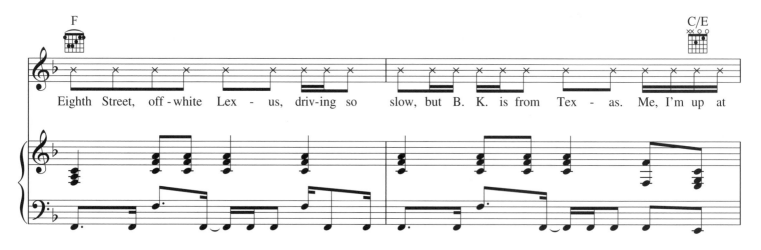

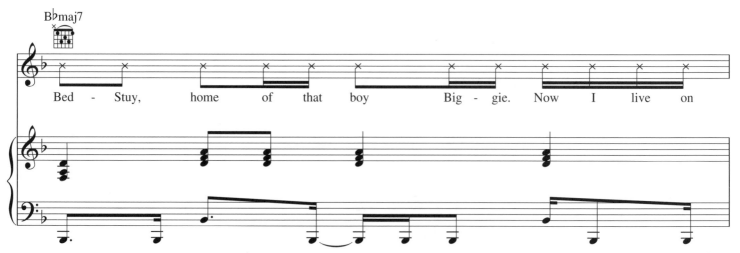

To Coda ⊕

re you.___ Let's here it for New ___ York, New ___ York, New ___

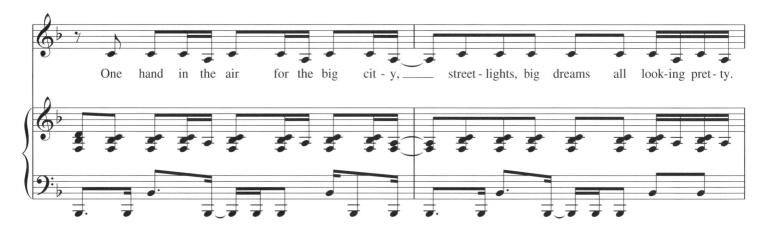

___ York. ___ Catch me at the ___ York. ___

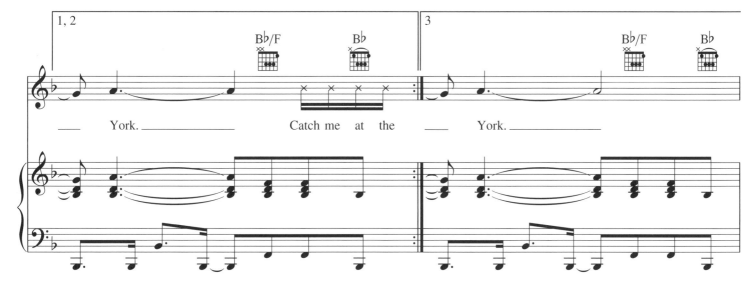

One hand in the air for the big cit-y,___ street-lights, big dreams all look-ing pret-ty.

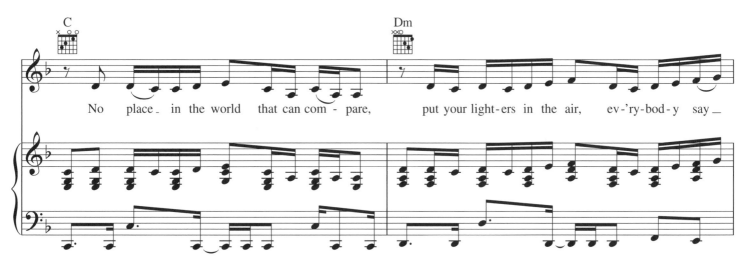

No place _ in the world that can com-pare, put your light-ers in the air, ev-'ry-bod-y say _

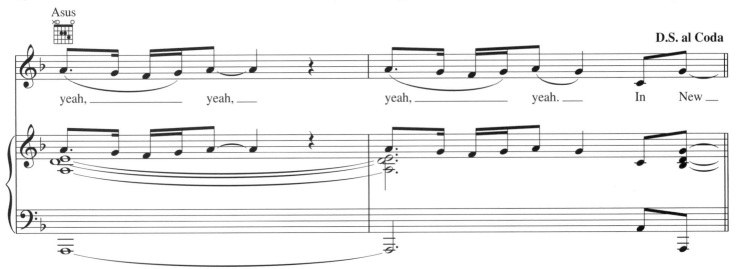

D.S. al Coda

yeah, _____ yeah, ___ yeah, _____ yeah. ___ In New ___

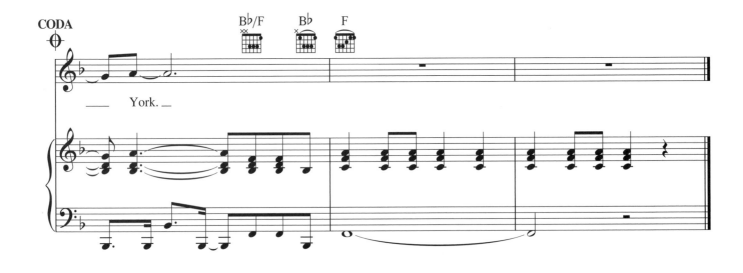

___ York. ___

Rap Lyrics

2. Catch me at the X with OG at a Yankee game.
   Dude, I made the Yankee hat more famous than a Yankee can.
   You should know I bleed blue, but I ain't a crip though,
   But I got a gang of brothas walking with my clique though.

   Welcome to the melting pot, corners where we selling rocks,
   Afrika bambaataa, home of the hip-hop,
   Yellow cab, gypsy cab, dollar cab, holla back,
   For foreigners it ain't for they act like they forgot how to act.

   Eight million stories out there and they're naked.
   City, it's a pity half of y'all won't make it.
   Me, I gotta plug Special Ed, I got it made,
   If Jeezy's paying LeBron, I'm paying Dwyane Wade.

   3 dice, Cee Lo, 3-Card Monte,
   Labor Day parade, rest in peace Bob Marley.
   Statue of Liberty, long live the World Trade,
   Long live the King, yo, I'm from the Empire State that's...

3. Lights is blinding, girls need blinders
   So they can step out of bounds quick.
   The sidelines is blind with casualties, who sip your life casually,
   Then gradually become worse. Don't bite the apple, Eve.

   Caught up in the in-crowd, now you're in style,
   And in the winter gets cold, en vogue with your skin out.
   The city of sin is a pity on a whim,
   Good girls gone bad, the city's filled with them.

   Mami took a bus trip, now she got her bust out,
   Everybody ride her, just like a bus route.
   Hail Mary to the city, you're a virgin,
   And Jesus can't save you, life starts when the church in.

   Came here for school, graduated to the high life.
   Ball players, rap stars, addicted to the limelight.
   MD, MA got you feeling like a champion,
   The city never sleeps, better slip you a Ambien.

BILLIONAIRE

Words and Music by TRAVIS McCOY,
PHILIP LAWRENCE, BRUNO MARS
and ARI LEVINE

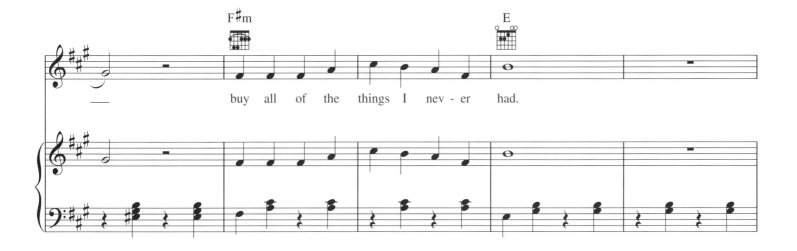

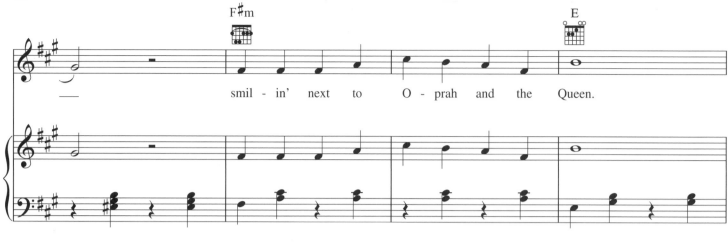

smil - in' next to O - prah and the Queen.

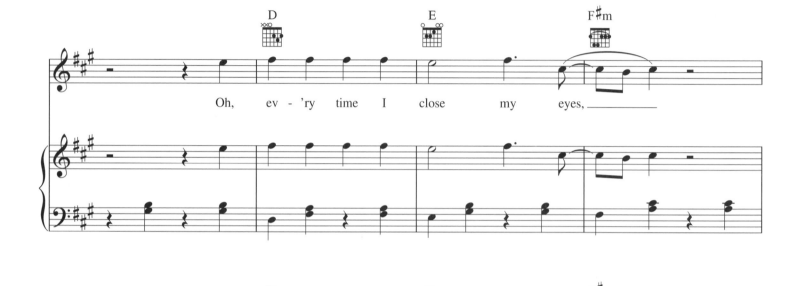

Oh, ev - 'ry time I close my eyes, _____

I see my name in shin - ing lights. _____

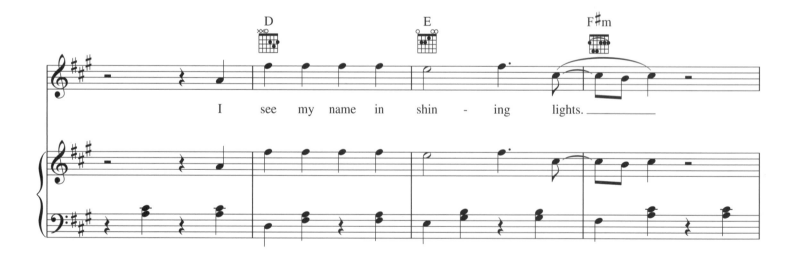

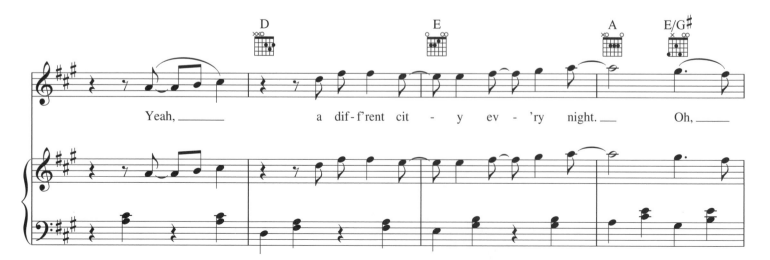

Yeah, _____ a dif-f'rent cit - y ev - 'ry night. _____ Oh, _____

I, _____ I _____ swear ___ the world ___ bet - ter ___ pre - pare ___

_____ for when I'm _____ a bil - lion - aire. _____

drum fill

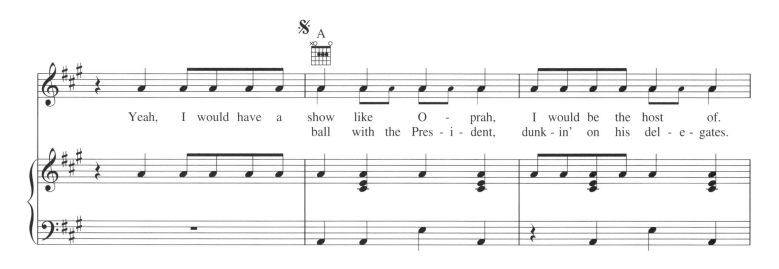

Yeah, I would have a show like O - prah, I would be the host of.
ball with the Pres - i - dent, dunk - in' on his del - e - gates.

Ev - 'ry day Christ - mas, give Art - ie a wish list.
Then I com - pli - ment him on his po - lit - i - cal et - i - quette.

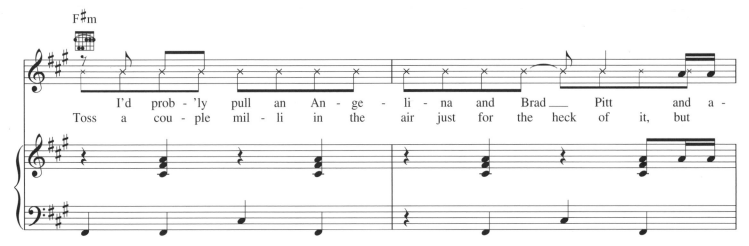

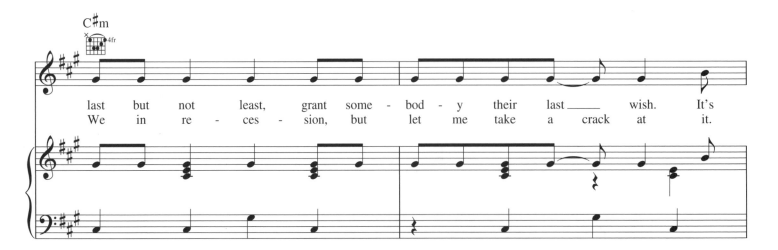

been a cou - ple months that I been sin - gle.____ So
I'll prob - 'ly take what - ev - er's left and just split it up

you can call me Art - ie Claus, mi - nus the Ho ____ Ho.
so ev - 'ry - bod - y that I love can have a cou - ple bucks.

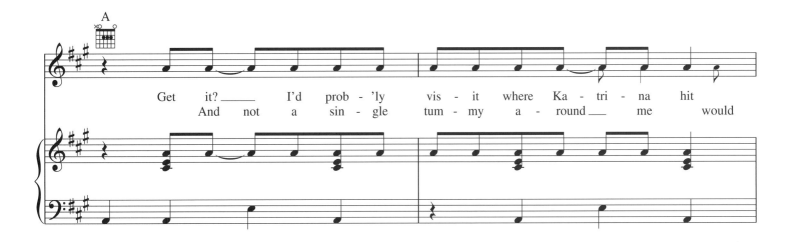

Get it? ____ I'd prob - 'ly vis - it where Ka - tri - na hit
And not a sin - gle tum - my a - round ____ me would

and darn sure do a lot more than FE - MA did.
know what hun - gry was, eat - in' good, sleep - in' sound - ly.

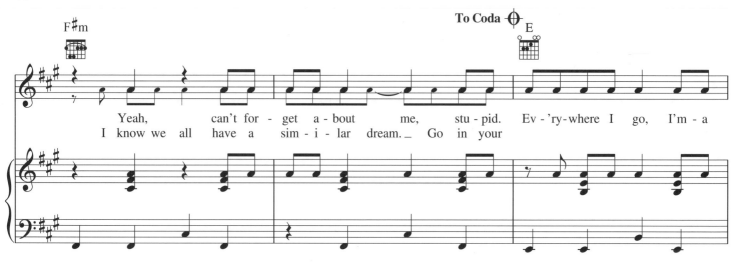

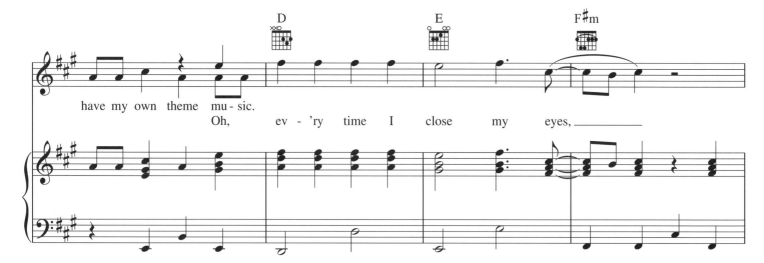

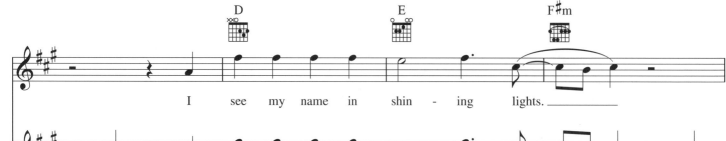

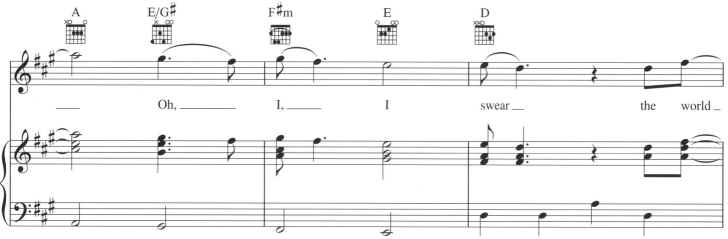

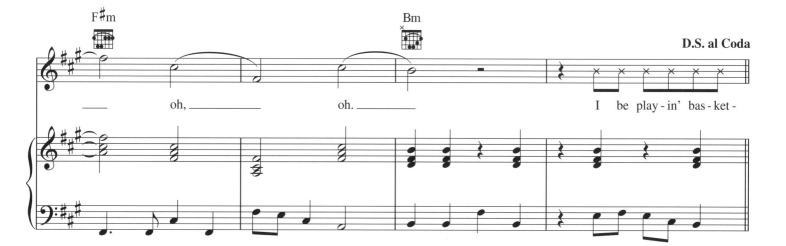

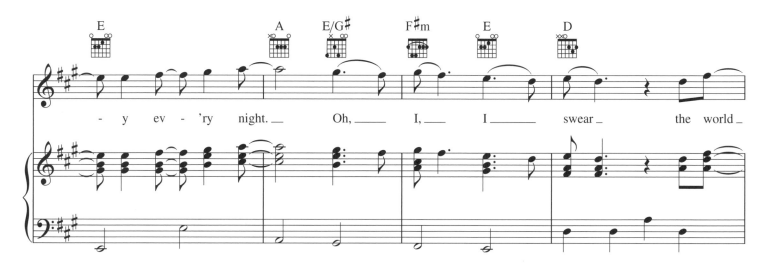

bet - ter ___ pre - pare ___ for when I'm ___ a bil - lion - aire, ___

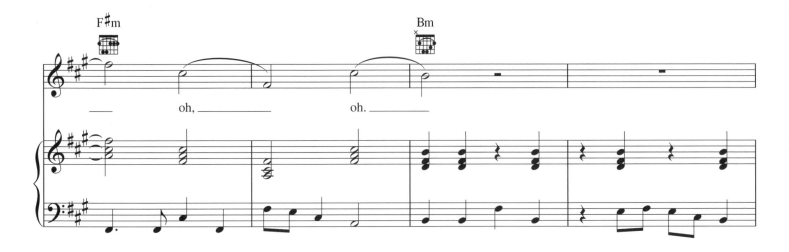

___ oh, ___ oh, ___ when I'm ___ a bil - lion - aire, ___

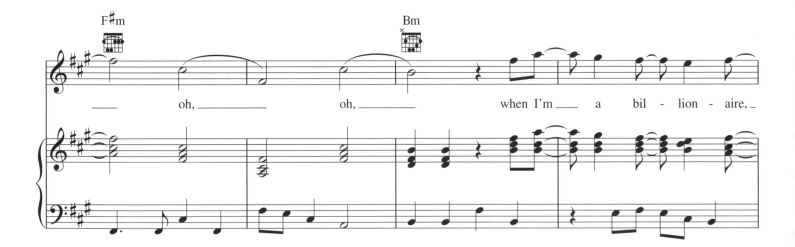

___ oh, ___ oh. ___

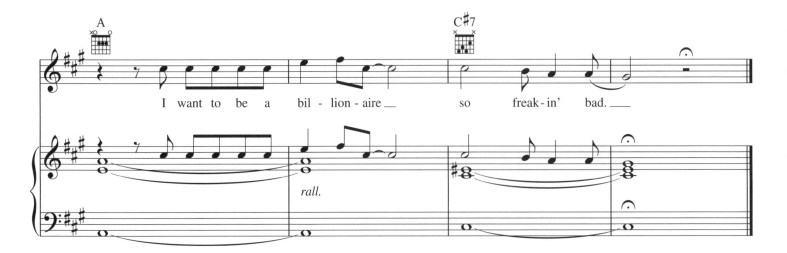

I want to be a bil - lion - aire ___ so freak - in' bad. ___

rall.

ME AGAINST THE MUSIC

Words and Music by TERIUS NASH, CHRISTOPHER STEWART,
DORIAN HARDNETT, GARY O'BRIEN, BRITNEY SPEARS,
THABISO NKHEREANYE and MADONNA CICCONE

Hey Brit - ney,   are you read - y?

Uh - huh.   Are you, uh?

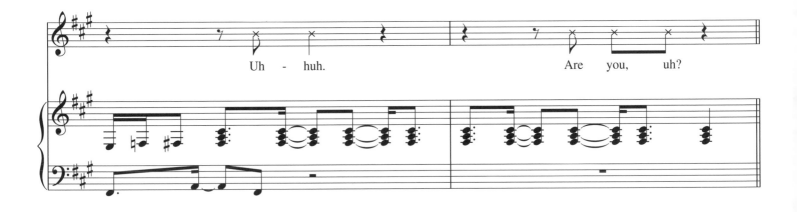

And no ___ one cares.   It's whip - pin' my hair, it's pull - in' my waist. ___
We're al - most there.   I'm feel - in' it bad and I can't ___ ex - plain. ___

To hell ___ with stares.   The sweat is drip - pin' all o - ver my face. ___
My soul ___ is bare.   My hips are mov - in' at a rap - id pace. ___

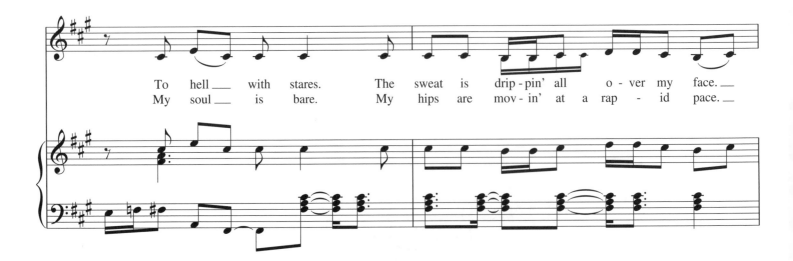

And no __ one's there. __ I'm the on - ly one danc - in' up in this place. __
Ba - by, feel __ it burn __ from the tip of my toes, run - nin' through my veins. __

To - night __ I'm here. __ Feel the beat of the drum, got - ta get with that bass. __ I'm
And now's __ your turn. __ Let me see what you got, don't hes - i - tate. __

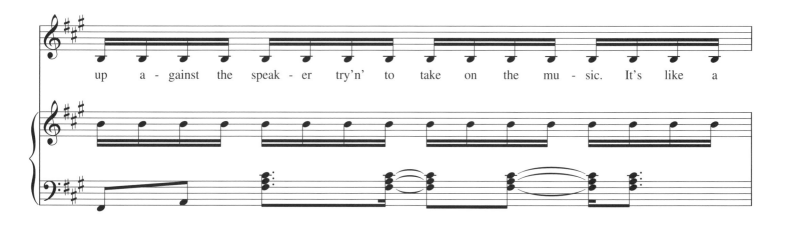

up a - gainst the speak - er try'n' to take on the mu - sic. It's like a

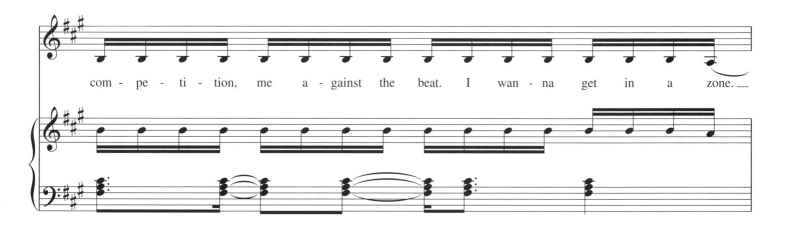

com - pe - ti - tion, me a - gainst the beat. I wan - na get in a zone. __

I wan-na get in a zone. ___ If you

real - ly wan-na bat - tle, sad - dle up and get your rhy - thm. Try'n' to

hit it, chic - a - ta. In a min - ute, I'm a take a you on. ___

N.C.

I'm a take a you on, ___ hey, hey, hey.

All my peo-ple on the floor, let me see you dance. Let me see ya.

All my peo-ple want-in' more, let me see you dance. I wan-na see ya.

All my peo-ple round and round, let me see you dance. Let me see ya.

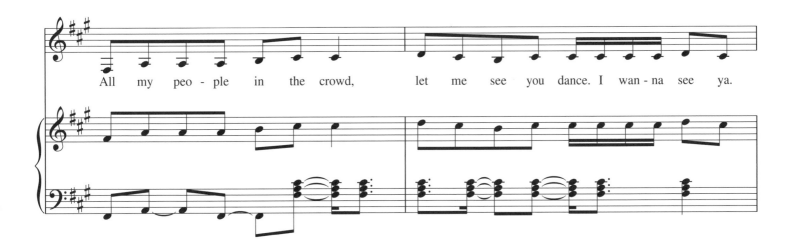

All my peo-ple in the crowd, let me see you dance. I wan-na see ya.

How would you like a friend - ly com - pe - ti - tion? Let's take on the song. ___ Let's

take on the song. ___ Let's take on your song. ___ It's

you and me, ba - by, we're the mu - sic. Time to par - ty all night long. ___

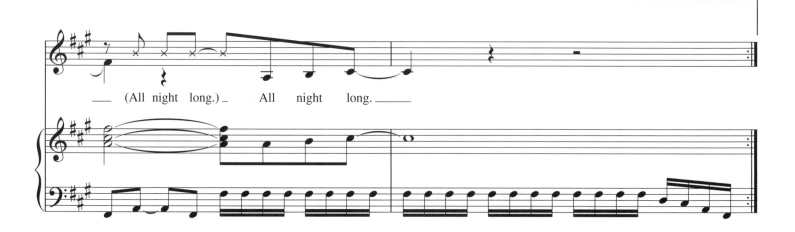

___ (All night long.) ___ All night long. ___

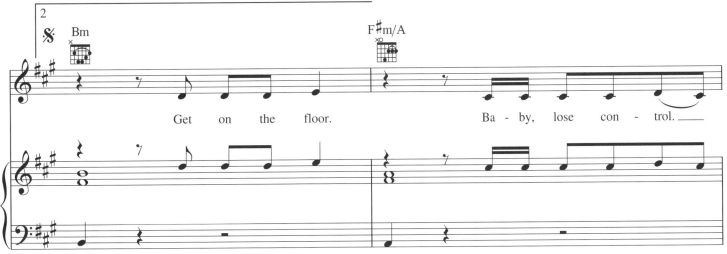

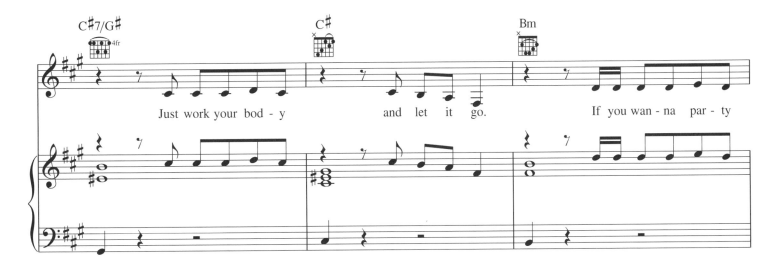

Come o-ver here, I got some-thin' to show ya. Sex-y la - dy,

I'd rath - er see you bare ____ your soul. If you

think you're so hot, bet - ter show me what you got. All my peo - ple in the crowd,

let me see you dance. Come on, Brit - ney, lose con - trol.

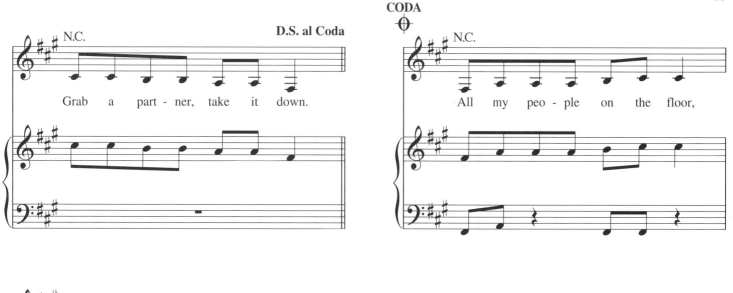

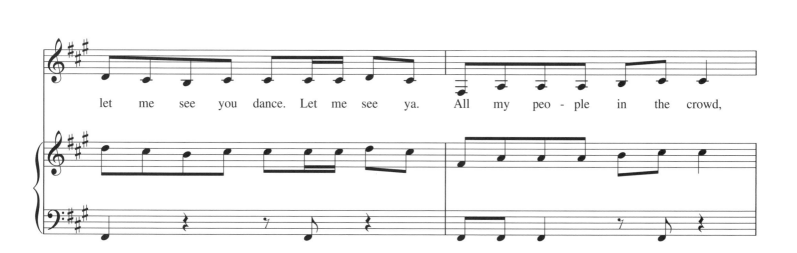

let me see you dance. I wan-na see ya. All my peo-ple in the crowd,

let me see you dance. Come on, Brit-ney, take it down. Make the mu-sic dance.

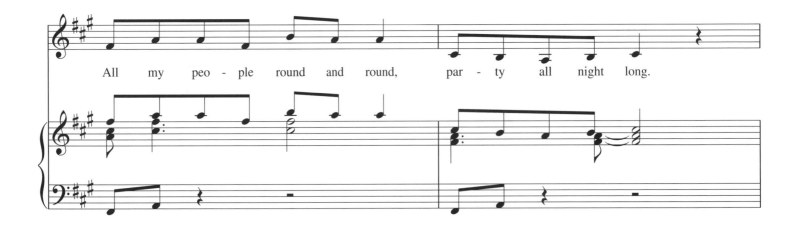

All my peo-ple round and round, par-ty all night long.

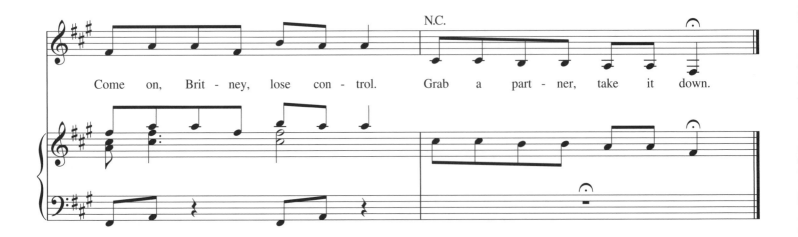

Come on, Brit-ney, lose con-trol. Grab a part-ner, take it down.

STRONGER

Words and Music by MARTIN SANDBERG
and RAMI YACOUB

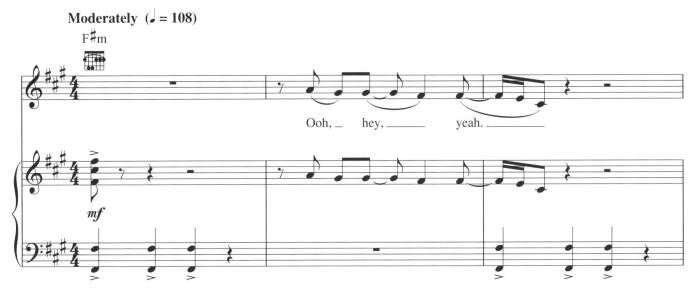

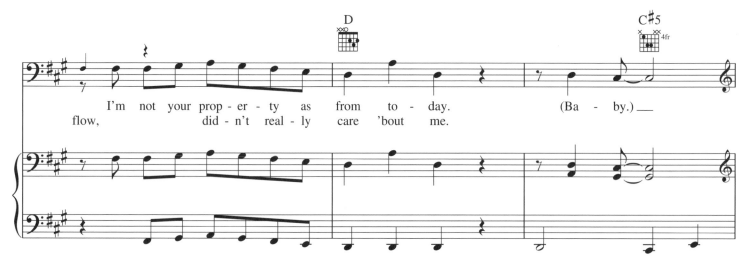

I'm not your prop-er-ty as from to-day. (Ba - by.) __
flow, did - n't real-ly care 'bout me.

You might think that I __ won't make __ it on my own. __
You might think that I __ can't take __ it, but you're wrong. __

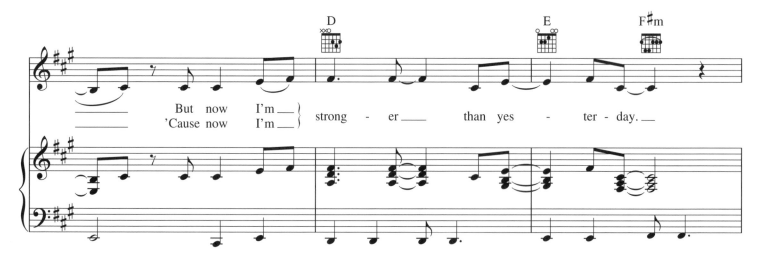

__ But now I'm __ } strong - er __ than yes - ter-day. __
__ 'Cause now I'm __ }

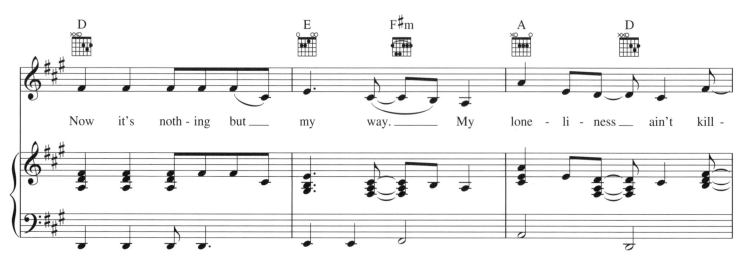

Now it's noth-ing but __ my way. __ My lone-li-ness __ ain't kill -

Here I go, _____ on my own __ now.

I don't need no-bod - y, not an-y-bod - y.

Here I go. _____

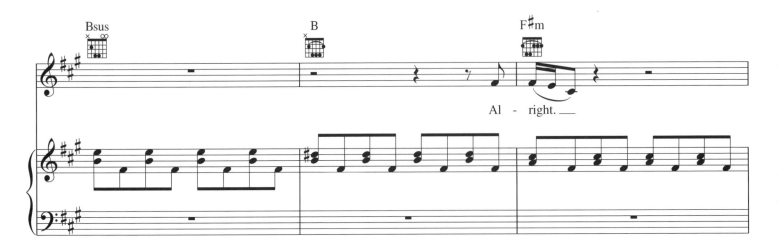

Al - right. __

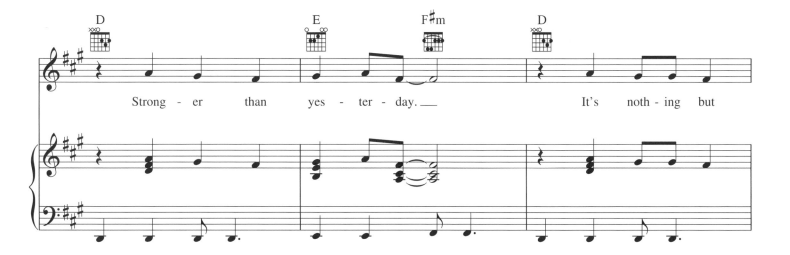

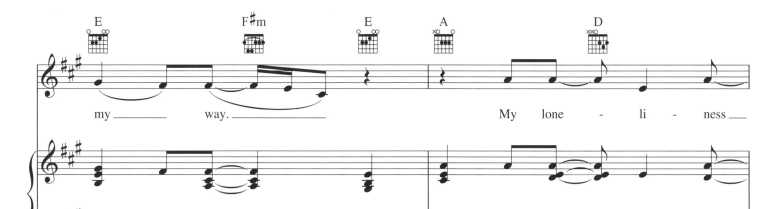

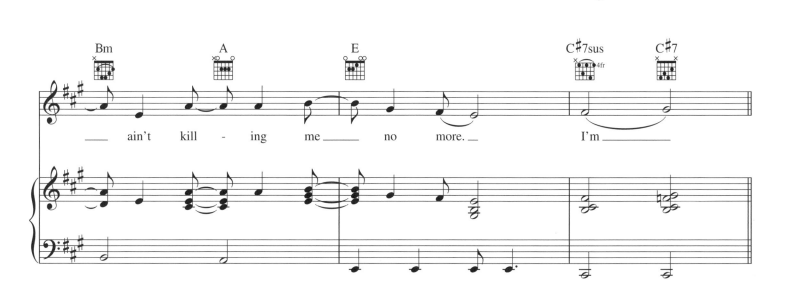

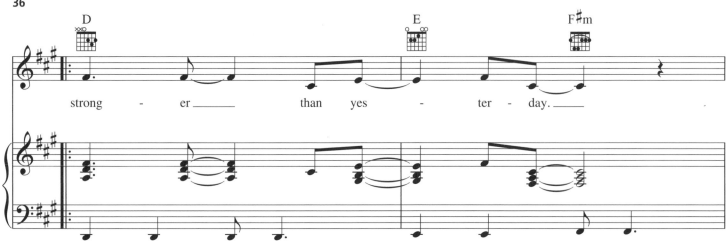

strong - er _____ than yes - ter - day. _____

Now it's noth - ing but ___ my way. _____ My lone - li - ness ___ ain't kill -

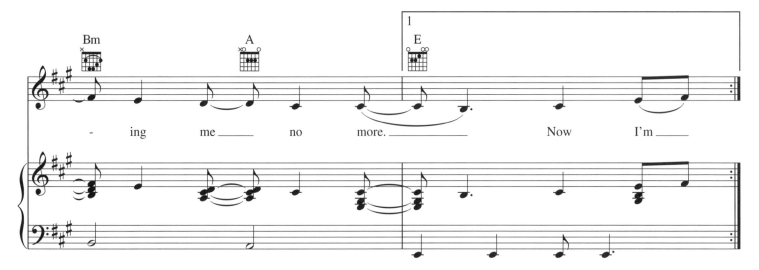

- ing me ____ no more. _____ Now I'm _____

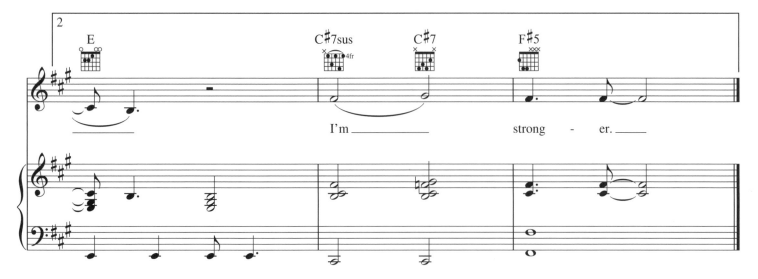

_____ I'm _____ strong - er. _____

TOXIC

Words and Music by CATHY DENNIS,
CHRISTIAN KARLSSON, PONTUS WINNBERG
and HENRIK JONBACK

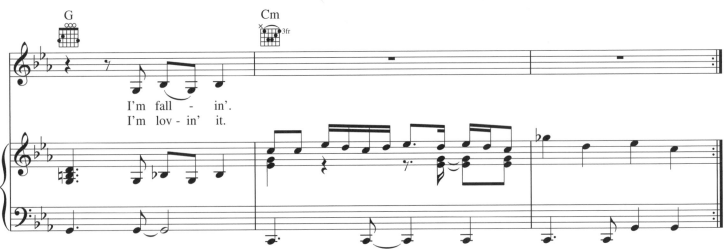

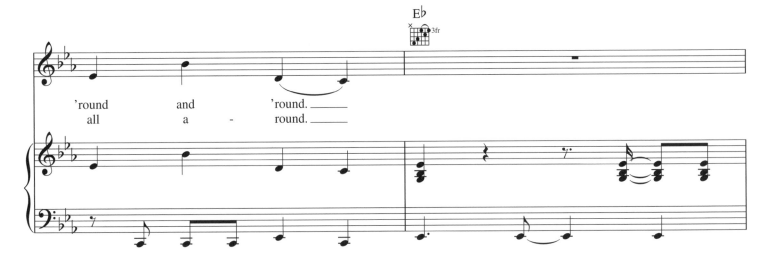

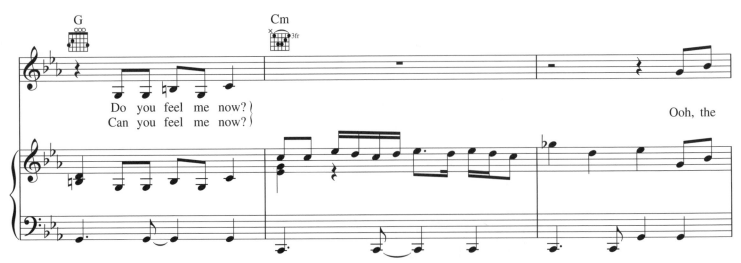

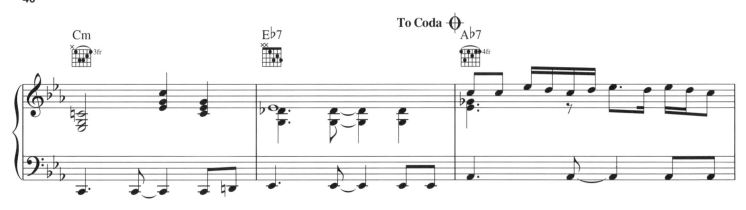

It's get - tin' late to give you up.

I took a sip from a dev - il's cup. Slow - ly,

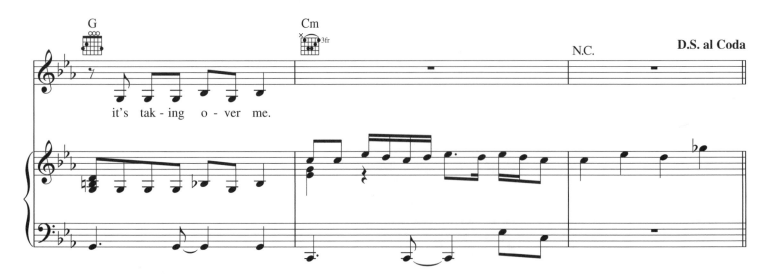

it's tak - ing o - ver me.

CODA

Don't you know that you're tox - ic? Taste of your lips, I'm

on a ride. You're tox - ic, I'm slip-pin' un - der. Ooh, the

taste of a poi - son par - a - dise. I'm ad - dict - ed to you. Don't you

know that you're tox - ic? Ooh, the taste of your lips, I'm on a ride.

THE ONLY EXCEPTION

Words and Music by HAYLEY WILLIAMS
and JOSH FARRO

Verse 1 (sing 1st time only):

1. When I was youn-ger, I saw my dad-dy cry____ and curse at the wind.__

Verse 2 (sing 2nd time only):

(2.) may-be I know some-where deep in my soul____ that love nev-er lasts.__

He broke his own heart, and I watched as he tried to re-

And we've got to find__ oth-er ways____ to make it a-lone,__

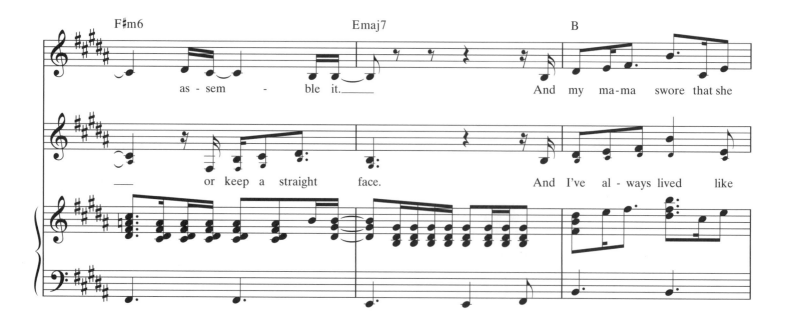

as-sem - ble it._____ And my ma-ma swore that she

____ or keep a straight face. And I've al-ways lived like

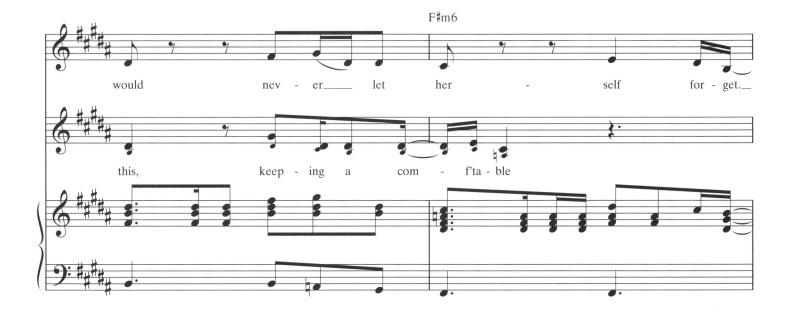

would nev - er___ let her - self for - get.___
this, keep - ing a com - f'ta - ble

___ dis - tance. And up un - til now I had sworn___
And that was the day___ that I

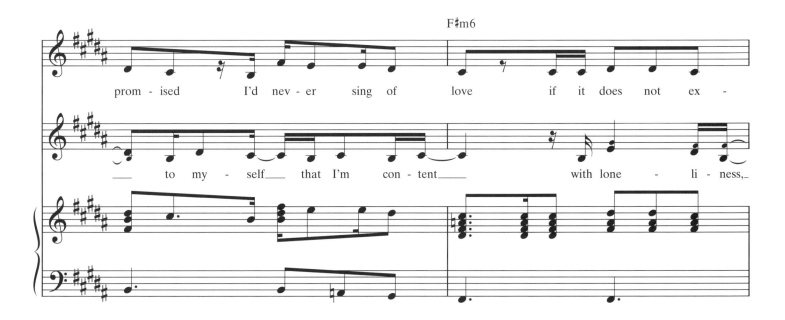

prom - ised I'd nev - er sing of love if it does not ex -
___ to my - self___ that I'm con - tent___ with lone - li - ness,___

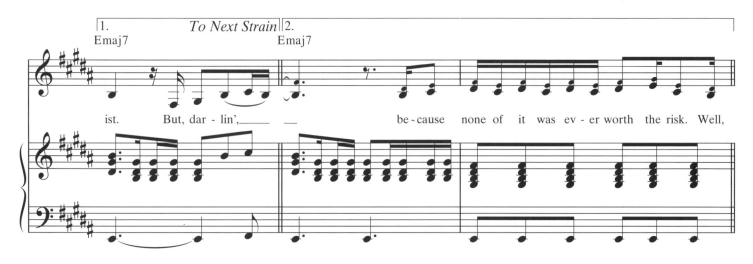

ist. But, dar - lin',_____ __ be - cause none of it was ev - er worth the risk. Well,

Chorus:

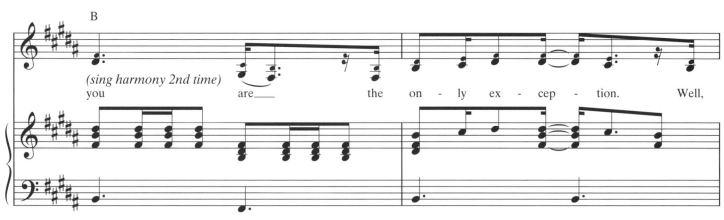

(sing harmony 2nd time)
you are_____ the on - ly ex - cep - tion. Well,

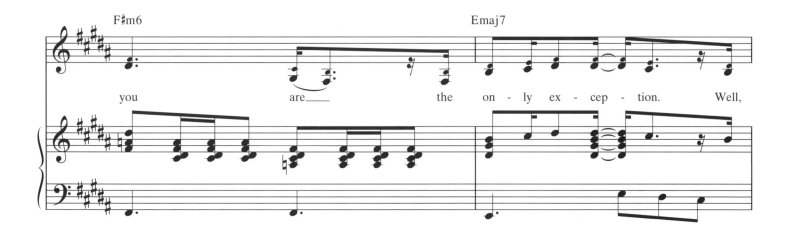

you are_____ the on - ly ex - cep - tion. Well,

you are_____ the on - ly ex - cep - tion. Well,

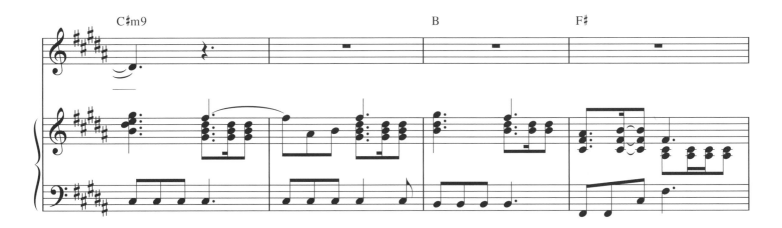

Bridge:

tight grip on re - al - i - ty, but I can't____ let

go of what's in front of me____ here.____ I know you're

leav - ing in the morn - ing when you wake up.____ Leave me

with some kind of proof it's not a dream.____ Oh.____

Chorus:

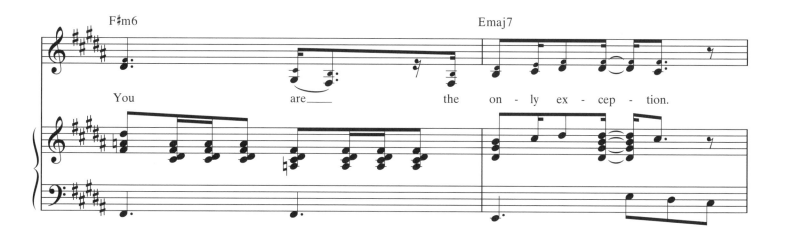

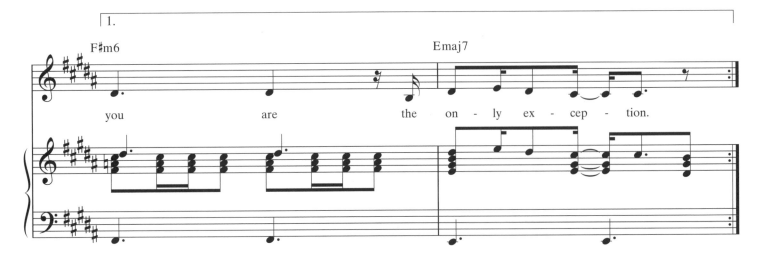

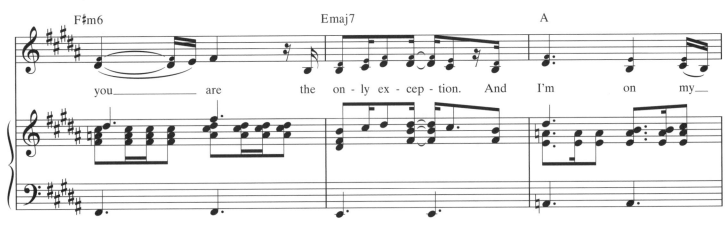

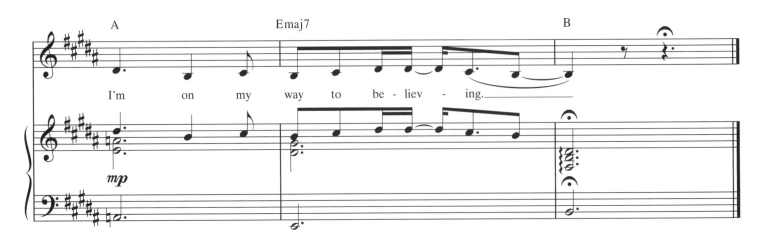

I WANT TO HOLD YOUR HAND

Words and Music by JOHN LENNON
and PAUL McCARTNEY

Gentle Folk

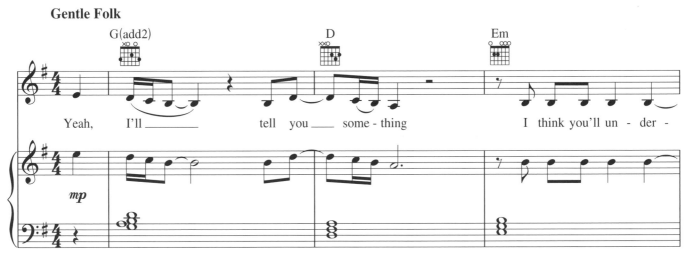

Yeah, I'll _____ tell you _____ some-thing I think you'll un - der -

- stand. When I _____ say that _____ some - thing,

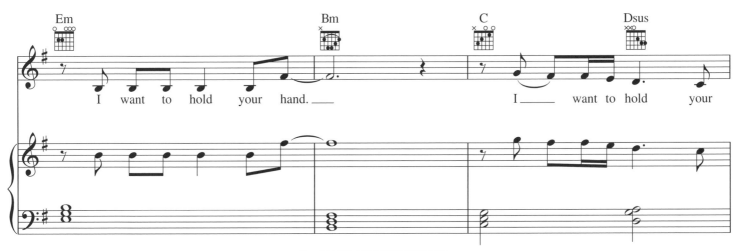

I want to hold your hand. _____ I _____ want to hold your

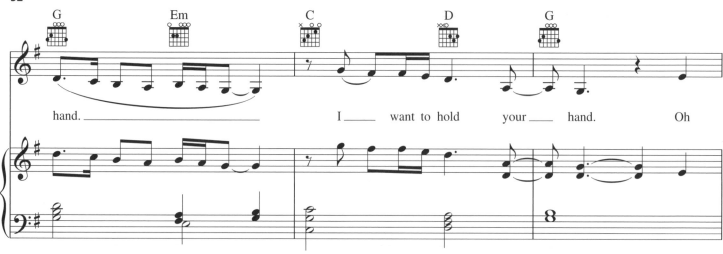

hand. _____ I _____ want to hold your _____ hand. Oh

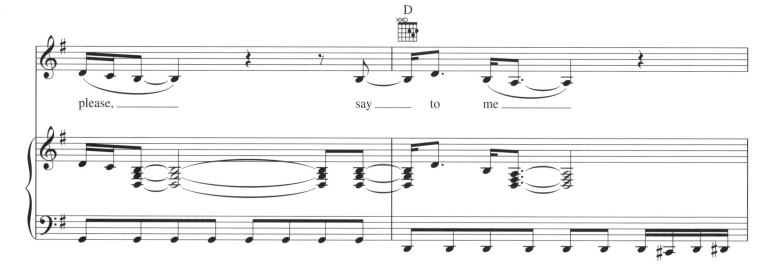

please, _____ say _____ to me _____

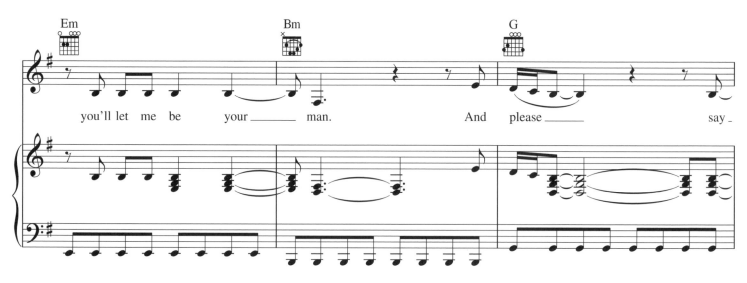

you'll let me be your _____ man. And please _____ say _

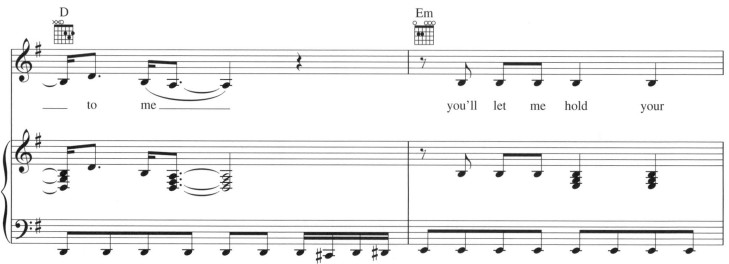

_____ to me _____ you'll let me hold your

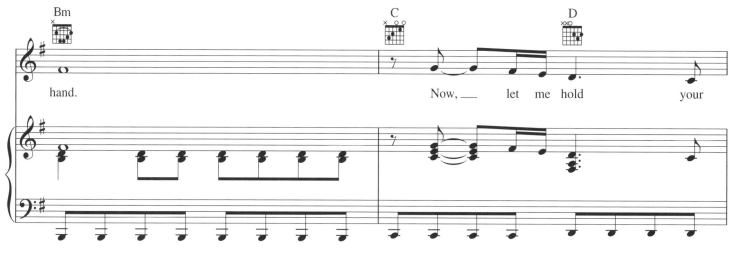

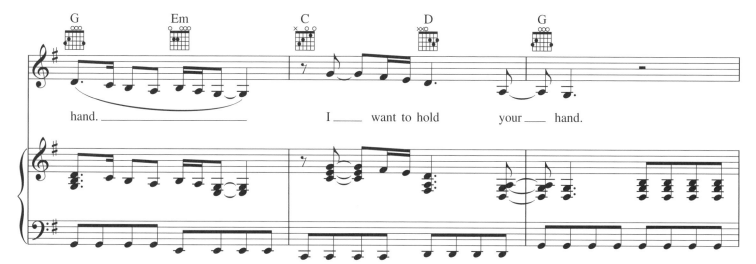

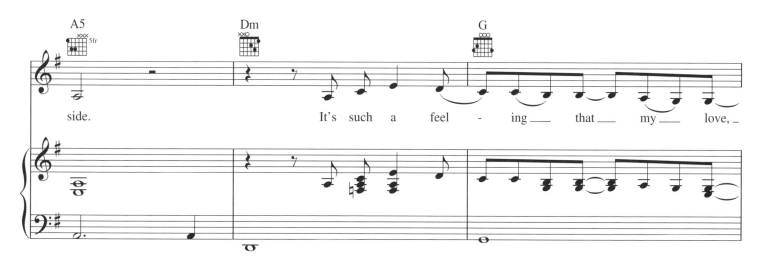

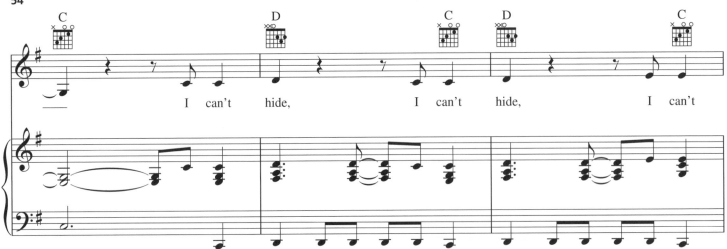

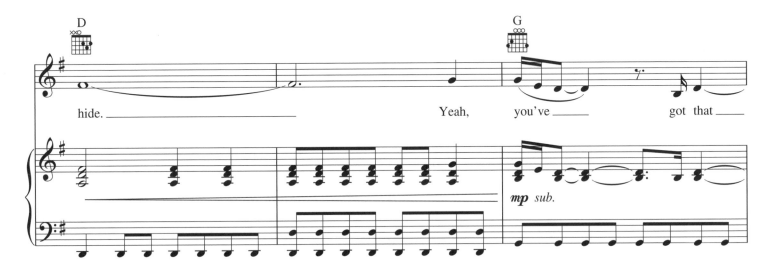

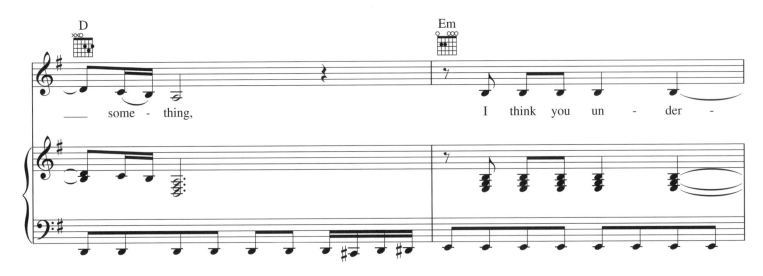

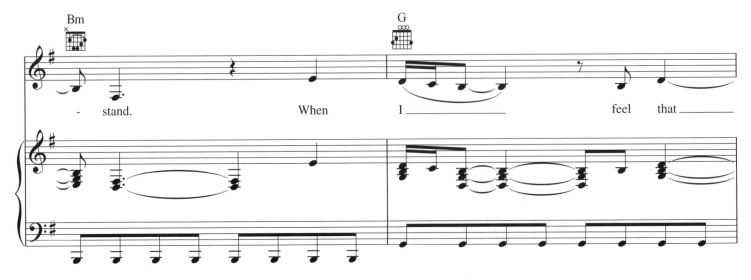

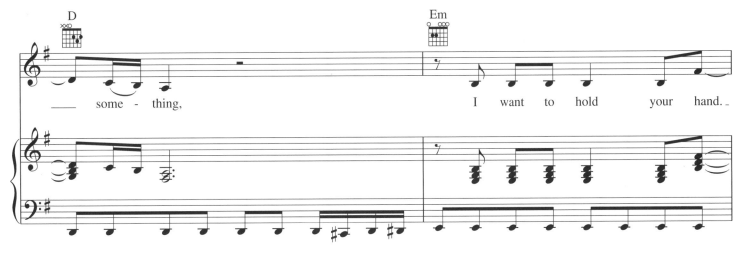

some - thing,   I want to hold your hand.

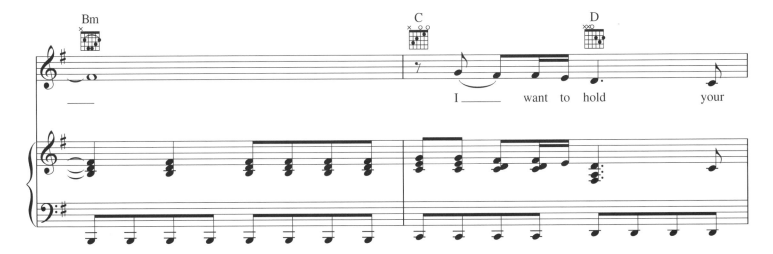

I _____ want to hold   your

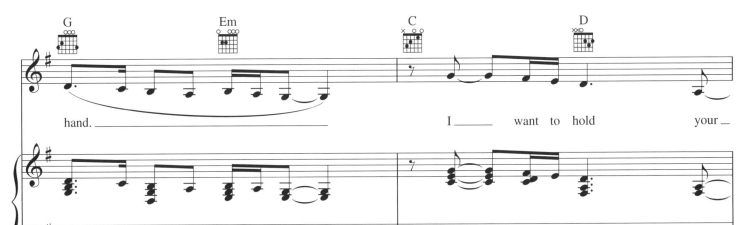

hand. _____   I _____ want to hold   your _

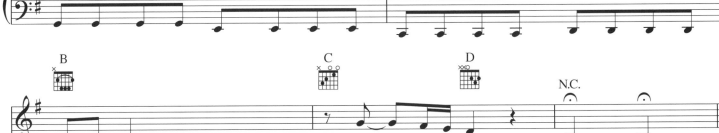

_____ hand. _   I _____ want to hold   your hand.

freely

ONE OF US

Words and Music by
ERIC BAZILIAN

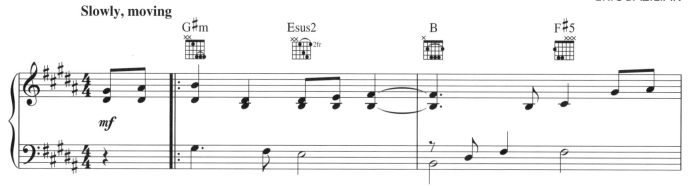

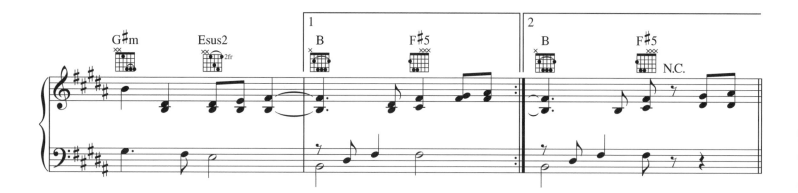

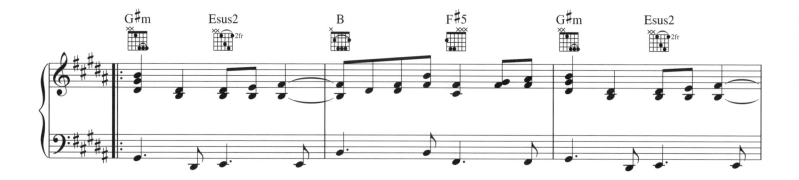

If God had a name, ___
God had a face, ___

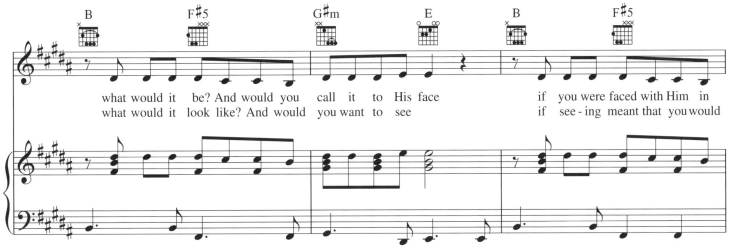

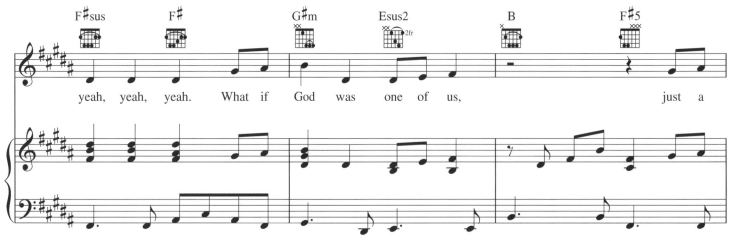

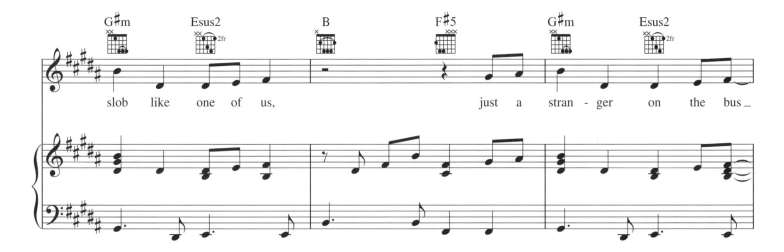

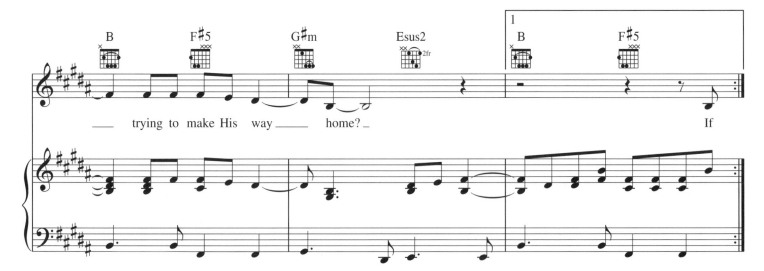

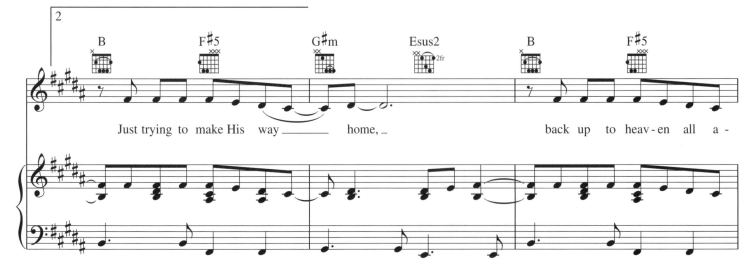

lone. No - bod - y call - ing on the phone,

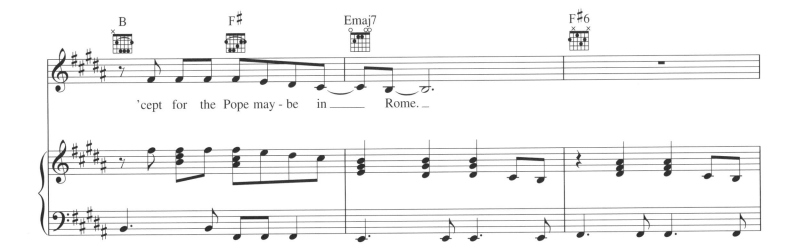

'cept for the Pope may - be in Rome.

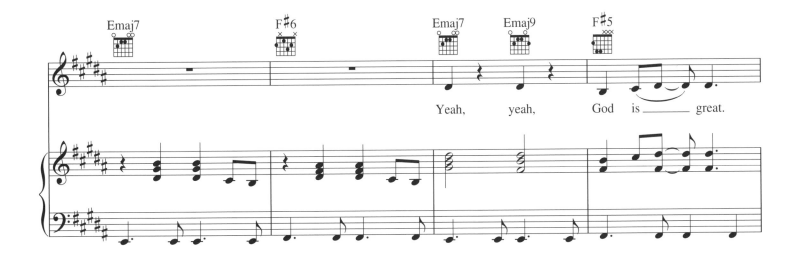

Yeah, yeah, God is great.

Yeah, yeah, God is good. Yeah, yeah,

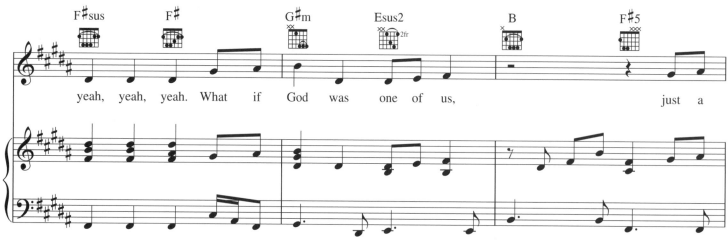

yeah, yeah, yeah. What if God was one of us, just a

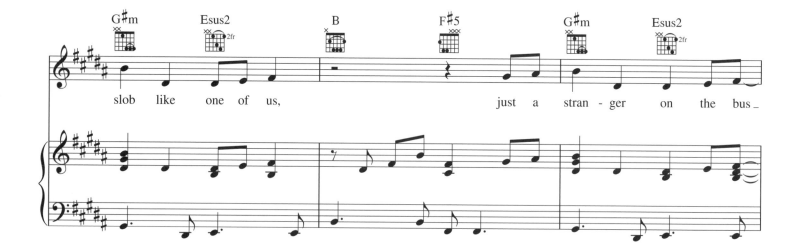

slob like one of us, just a stran-ger on the bus

trying to make His way home, just trying to make His way

home, just like a ho-ly roll-ing stone?

Back up to heav-en all a - lone,

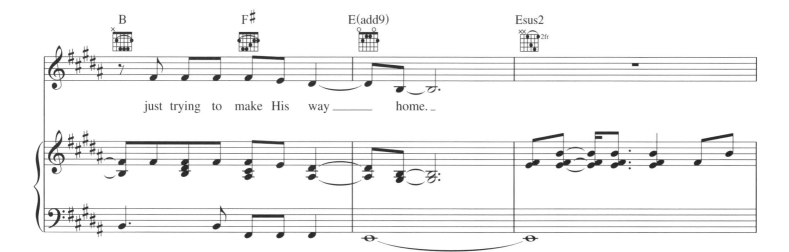

just trying to make His way _____ home. _

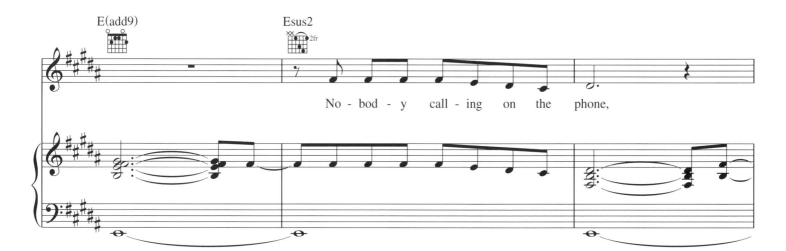

No - bod - y call - ing on the phone,

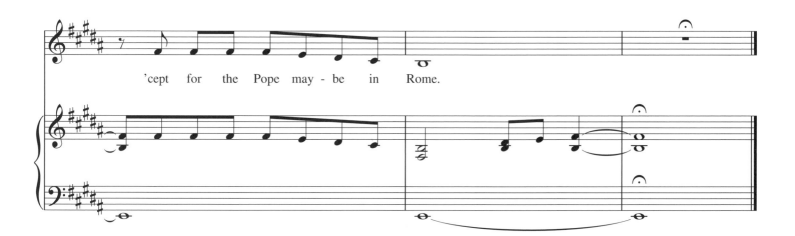

'cept for the Pope may - be in Rome.

RIVER DEEP - MOUNTAIN HIGH

Words and Music by JEFF BARRY,
ELLIE GREENWICH and PHIL SPECTOR

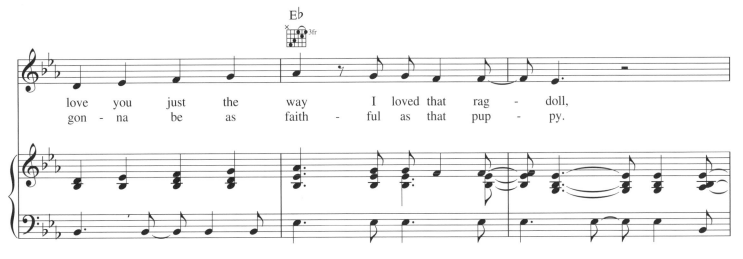

love you just the way I loved that rag - doll,
gon - na be as way faith - ful as that pup - py.

but on - ly now ___ my love ___ has grown. ___
You know I'll nev - er let ___ you down. ___

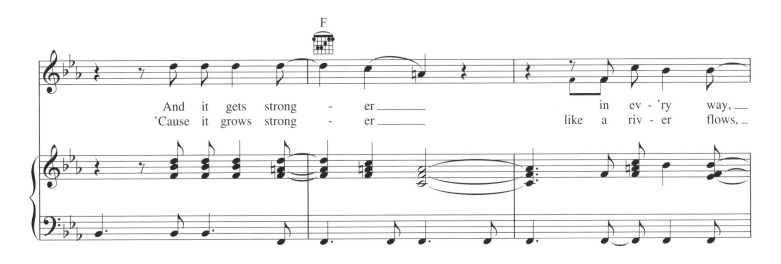

And it gets strong - er _____ in ev - 'ry way, ___
'Cause it grows strong - er _____ like a riv - er flows, _

___ and it gets deep - er,
___ and it gets big - ger,

let me say, ____

and heav - en knows, _

and it gets high -

and it gets sweet -

- er, ____

- er, ba - by,

day by day.

as it grows.

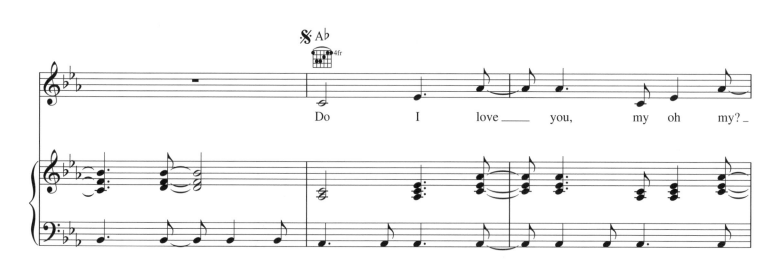

Do I love ____ you, my oh my?

Riv - er deep, _

moun - tain high. ____

Ab

If I lost ____ you, would I cry? ____

Bb

Oh, how I love you, ba - by, ____

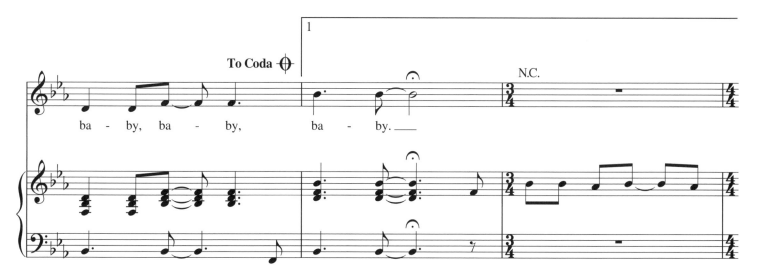

To Coda ⊕ | 1

N.C.

ba - by, ba - by, ba - by. ____

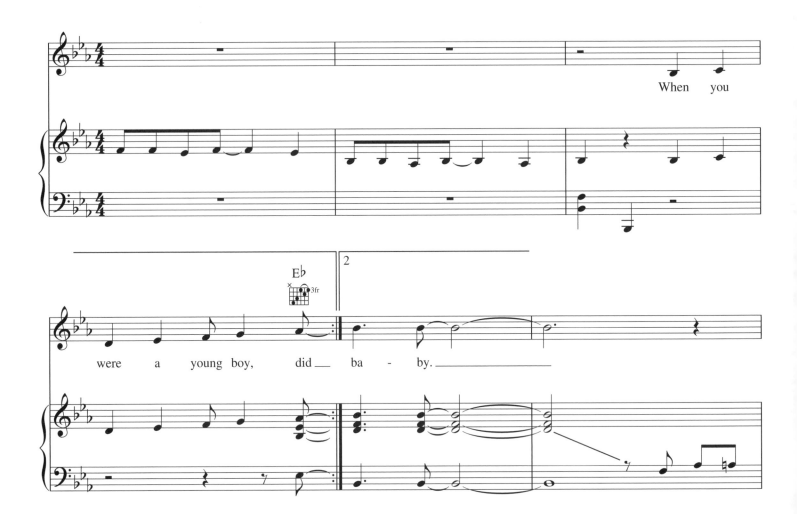

When you were a young boy, did __ ba - by. __

I love you, ba - by like __ a flow -

-er loves _ the spring; _ and I love you, ba -

-by, like _ the rob - in loves _ to sing. _

I love you, ba - by, like _ a school - boy loves his

pie; and I love you, ba - by, riv - er deep

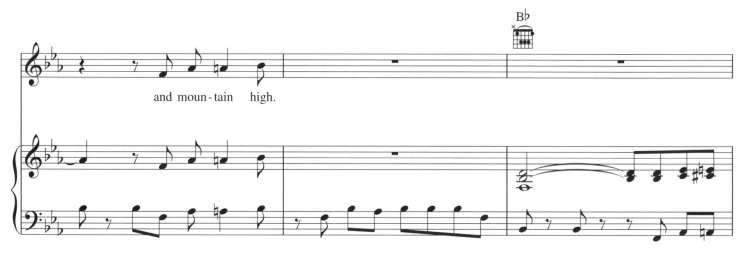

and moun-tain high.

D.S. al Coda

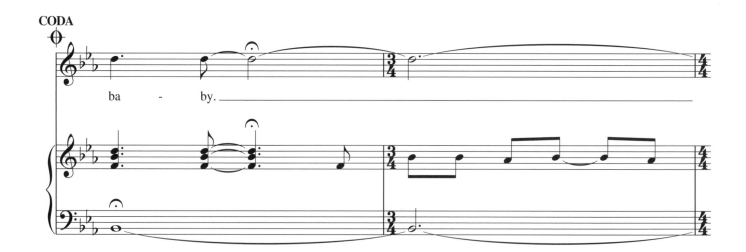

CODA

ba - by. _____

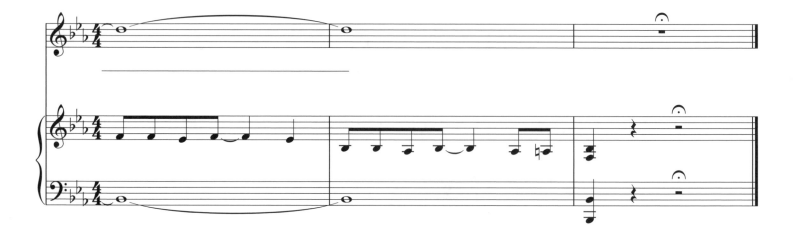

LUCKY

Words and Music by JASON MRAZ,
COLBIE CAILLAT and TIMOTHY FAGAN

*Substitute half rest on D.S.

D.S. al Coda

world keeps __ spin-ning 'round, you hold _____ me right __ here, right now.

CODA

Oo, _____

oo. _____ Oo, _____

_____ oo. _____ Oo. _____

ONE LOVE

Words and Music by
BOB MARLEY

Relaxed Reggae beat

One love, ___ one heart. ___

Let's get to-geth - er and feel all right.
{ As it was in the be-
I'm plead-ing to ___

To Coda ⊕

cry - ing. (One love.) ___ Hear the chil-dren cry - ing. (One heart.) ___ Say- in',
gin - ning, (One love.) ___ so shall it be in the end. ___ (One heart.) ___ Al- right,
man - kind. (One love.) ___ Oh, Lord. ___ (One heart.) ___ Whoa.
{ "Give

thanks and praise to the Lord and I will feel all right." Say - in',

"Let's get to - geth - er and feel all right." Whoa, whoa, whoa, whoa.
One more thing.

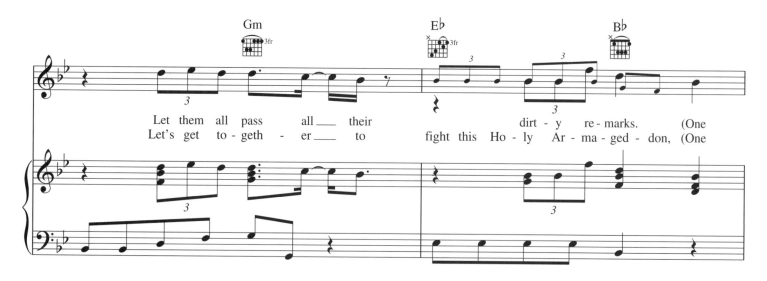

Let them all pass all ___ their dirt - y re - marks. (One
Let's get to - geth - er ___ to fight this Ho - ly Ar - ma - ged - don, (One

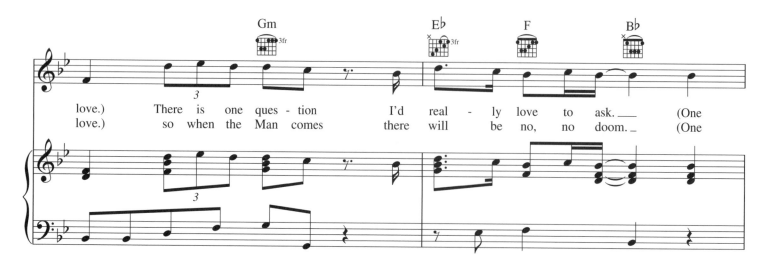

love.) There is one ques - tion I'd real - ly love to ask. ___ (One
love.) so when the Man comes there will be no, no doom. _ (One

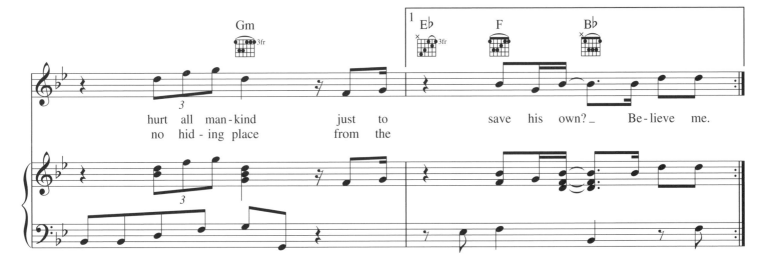

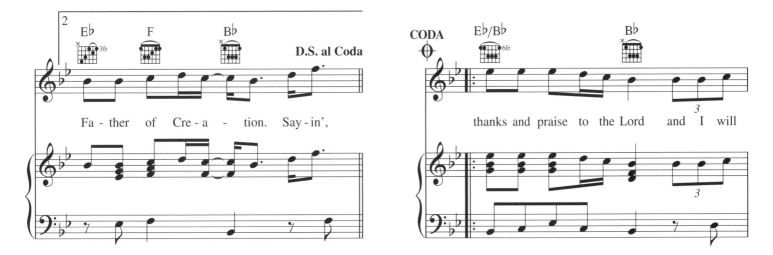

TEENAGE DREAM

Words and Music by LUKASZ GOTTWALD,
MAX MARTIN, BENJAMIN LEVIN,
BONNIE McKEE and KATY PERRY

Moderate Dance beat

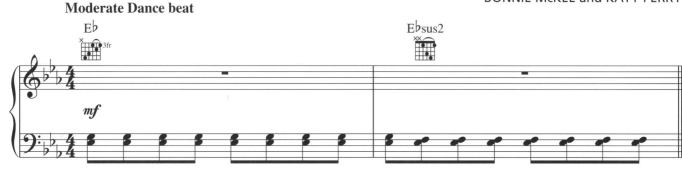

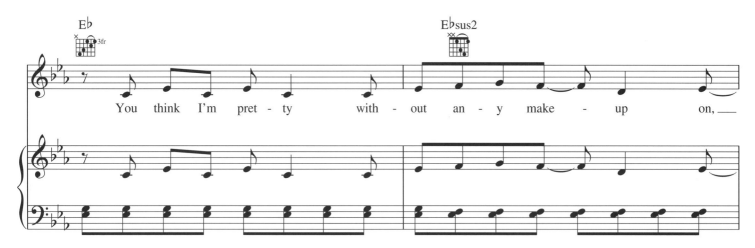

You think I'm pret-ty with-out an-y make - up on, ___

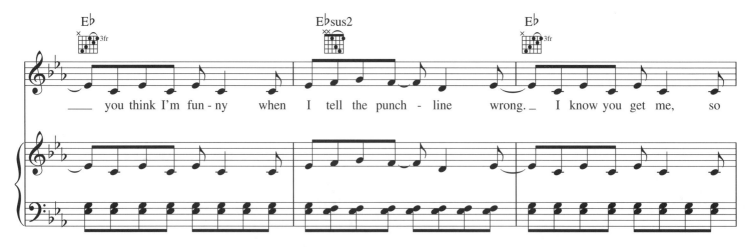

___ you think I'm fun-ny when I tell the punch - line wrong. ___ I know you get me, so

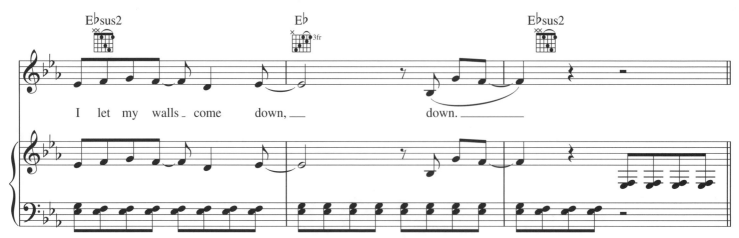

I let my walls ___ come down, ___ down. ___

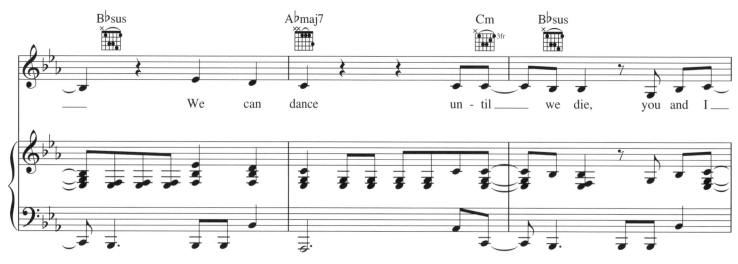

We can dance un - til ___ we die, you and I ___

will be young ___ for - ev - er. You make ___ me

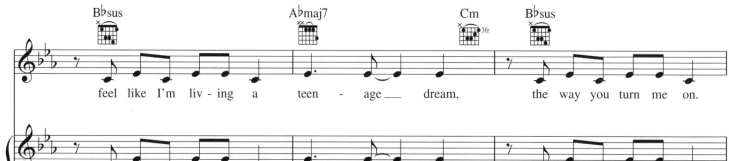

feel like I'm liv - ing a teen - age ___ dream, the way you turn me on.

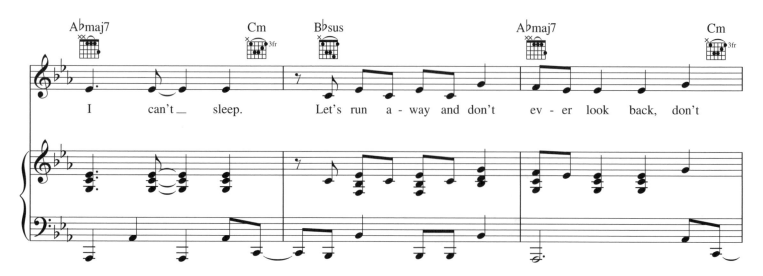

I can't ___ sleep. Let's run a - way and don't ev - er look back, don't

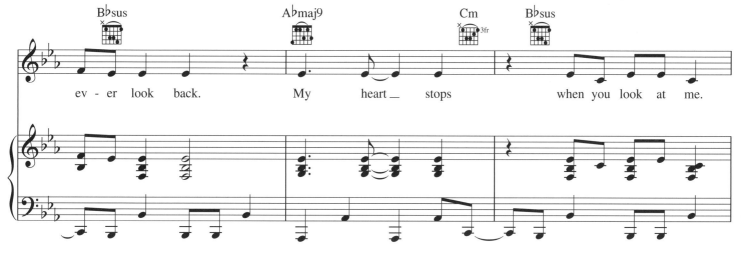

ev - er look back. My heart ___ stops when you look at me.

Just one ___ touch, now ba - by, I be - lieve this is ___ real.

So take a chance and don't ev - er look back, don't ev - er look back.

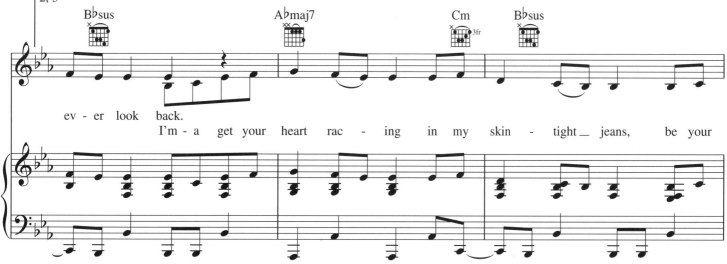

ev - er look back. I'm - a get your heart rac - ing in my skin - tight ___ jeans, be your

FORGET YOU

Words and Music by BRUNO MARS,
ARI LEVINE, PHILIP LAWRENCE,
THOMAS CALLAWAY and BRODY BROWN

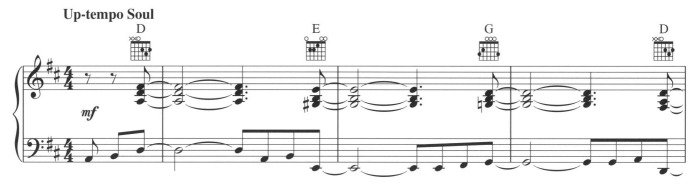

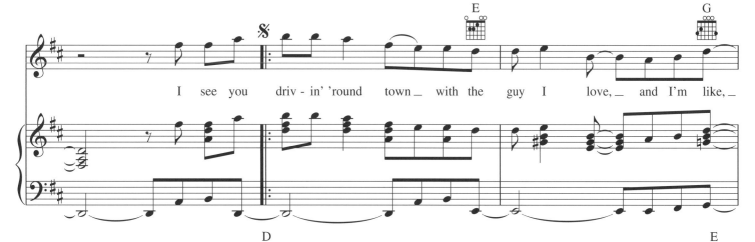

I see you driv-in' 'round town with the guy I love, and I'm like, for-get you.

I guess the change in my pock-et

was-n't e-nough. I'm like, for-get you and for-get him, too. Said if

but that don't mean I can't get you there. ___
beg and steal ___ and lie and cheat ___

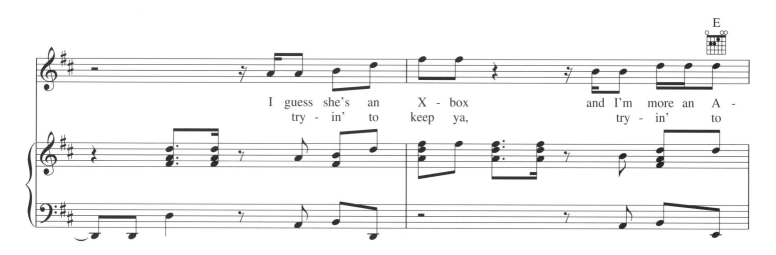

I guess she's an X - box
try - in' to keep ya,
and I'm more an A -
try - in' to

tar - i,
please ya.
but the way you play your game ain't fair. ___
'Cause ___ be - ing in love ___ with your ass ain't cheap.

I pit - y the fool _____ that

CODA

Now, ba - by, ba - by, ba - by, why you

wan - na, wan - na hurt me so bad? _____ (So bad, ___ so bad, ___

___ so bad.) _____ I tried to tell my ma - ma, but she

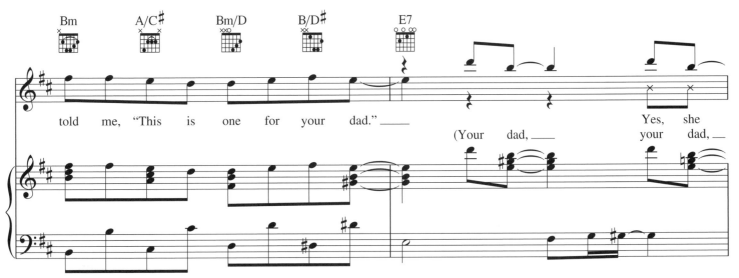

told me, "This is one for your dad." ___

(Your dad, ___ your dad, ___

Yes, she

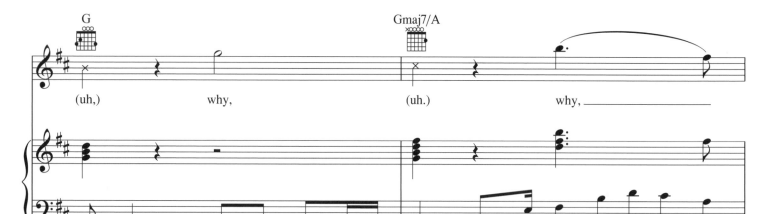

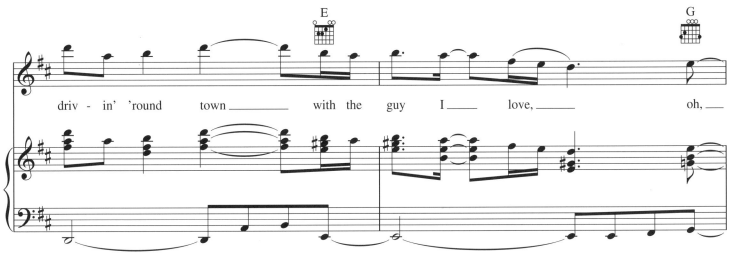

driv - in' 'round town _____ with the guy I ____ love, _____ oh, ____

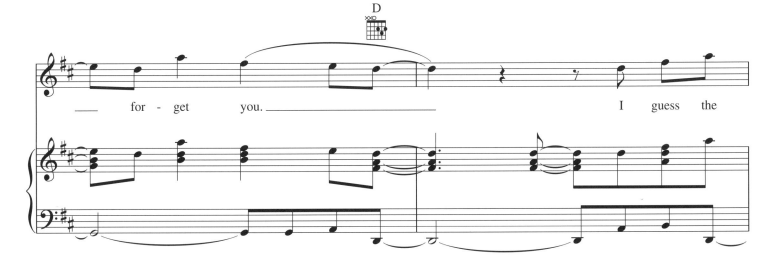

____ for - get you. _____ I guess the

change in my pock - et _____ was - n't e - nough. ___ I'm like

for - get you and for - get ____ him, too. ____ Said if

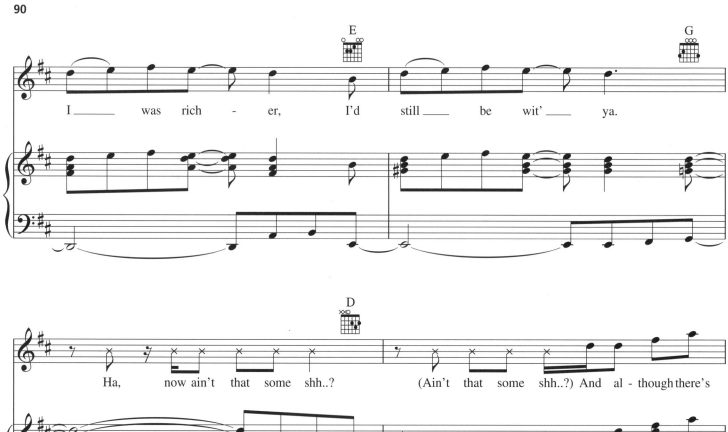

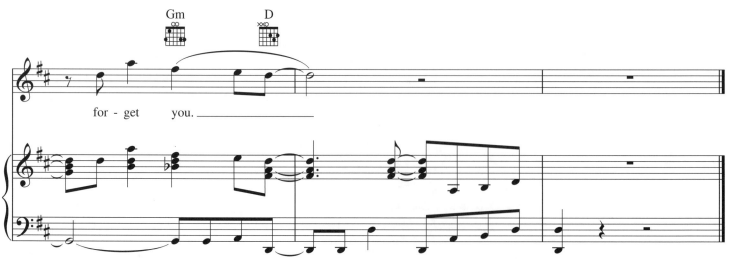

MARRY YOU

Words and Music by BRUNO MARS,
ARI LEVINE and PHILIP LAWRENCE

Moderately fast

Male: It's a beau-ti-ful night. _

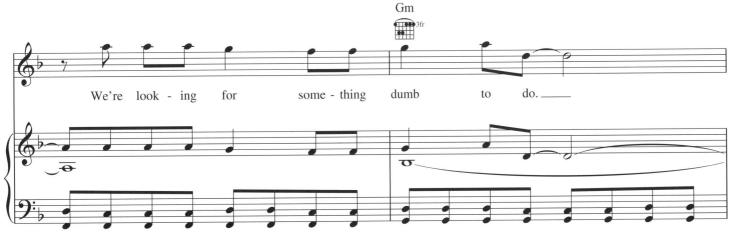

We're look-ing for some-thing dumb to do. _____

* Male lead vocals sung one octave lower than written.

Hey, ba - by, I think I wan - na mar - ry you.

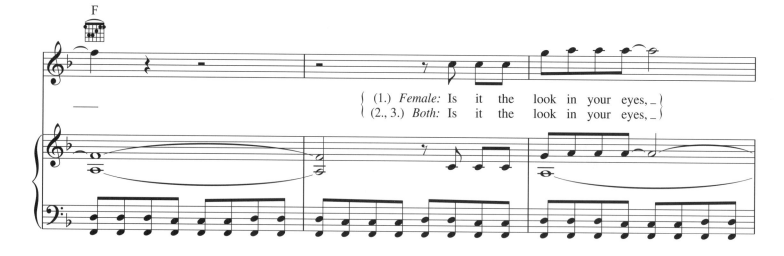

(1.) *Female:* Is it the look in your eyes,
(2., 3.) *Both:* Is it the look in your eyes,

or is it this danc - ing juice? Who cares,

ba - by; I think I wan - na mar - ry you.

Well, I know this lit - tle chap - el on the boul - e - vard. We can
I'll go get a ring; let the choir_ bells_ sing, like,_

Gm

go,_
"Ooh."_

no_ one will know._
So, what_ you wan - na do?_

Bb

F

Male: Oh, come on,_____ girl. ___ *Female:* Who
Male: Let's just run,_____ girl. ___

cares if we're trashed, got a pock - et full of cash we can
Both: If we wake_ up and we wan - na break_ up, that's_

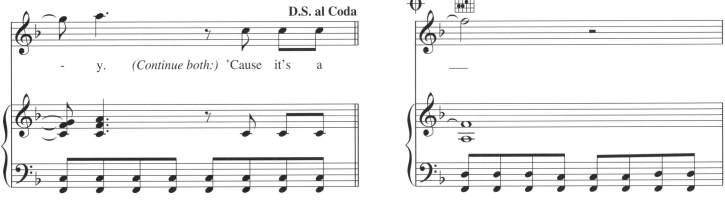

Tell __ me right now, ba - by.

Tell __ me right now, ba - by. Ba - by, just say, __ "I do." __

by, *Both:* oh, ____ 'cause it's a beau - ti - ful night. __

We're look - ing for some-thing dumb to do. __   Hey, ba -

SWAY
(Quien Sera)

English Words by NORMAN GIMBEL
Spanish Words and Music by PABLO BELTRAN RUIZ

When ma - rim - ba rhy - thms start to play, dance with me, make me sway.___ Like the la - zy o - cean hugs the shore, hold me close, sway me more._____ Like a flow - er bend - ing

JUST THE WAY YOU ARE

Words and Music by BRUNO MARS,
ARI LEVINE, PHILIP LAWRENCE,
KHARI CAIN and KHALIL WALTON

Moderate Hip-Hop groove

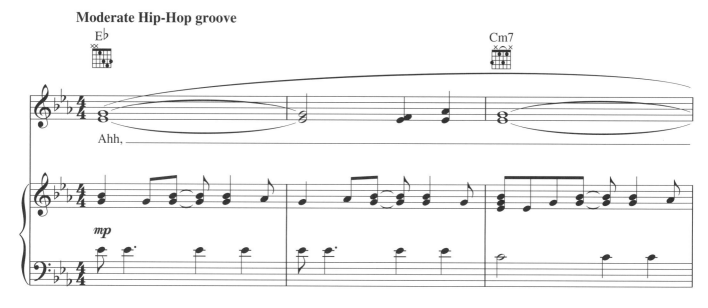

Ahh,

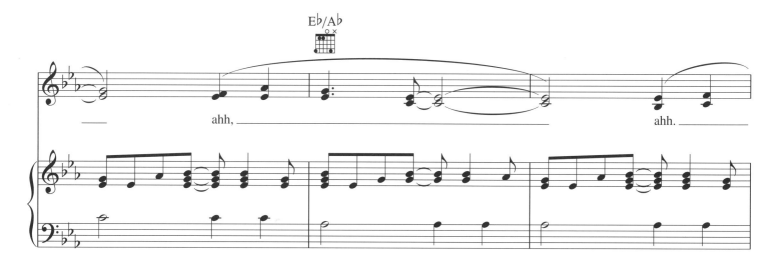

ahh, _____ ahh. _____

Oh, _____ her eyes, _ her eyes_ make the

stars look _ like they're _ not shin-in'. Her hair, _ her hair _ falls per-fect-ly ___ with-out _ her try - in'.

She's so beau - ti - ful, __ and I tell her ev - 'ry ____ day. _____

Yeah. I know, _ I know _ when I com-pli-ment _ her, she won't be - lieve _ me.

And it's so, ___ it's so ____ sad to think that she _ don't see _ what I _ see.

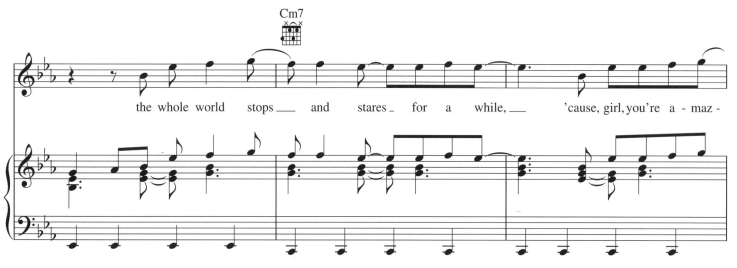

the whole world stops __ and stares __ for a while, __ 'cause, girl, you're a - maz-

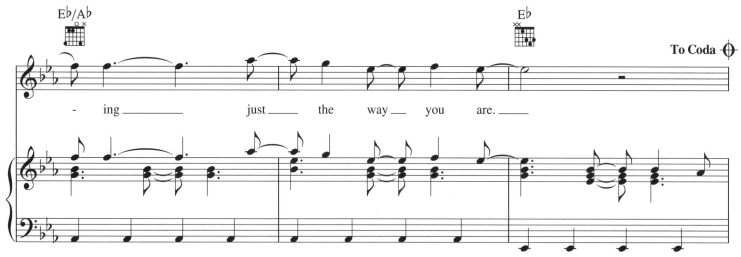

-ing _____ just ___ the way ___ you are. __

Yeah. __ Her lips, _ her lips, _ I could kiss them all __ day if __ she'd let me.

Her laugh, _ her laugh, _ she hates but I ___ think it's __ so sex - y. She's so beau - ti - ful, _

CODA

The way you are, the way you are.

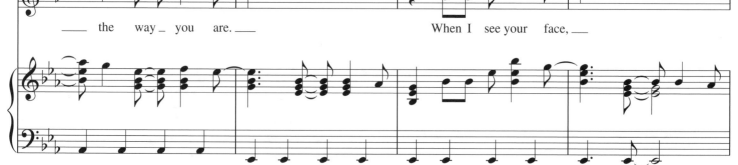

Cm7 Eb/Ab

the way you are. Girl, you're a-maz - ing just

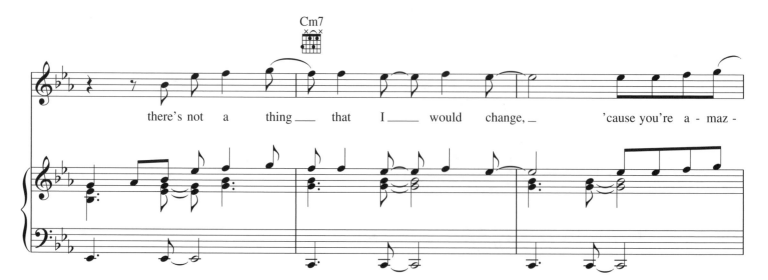

Eb

the way you are. When I see your face,

Cm7

there's not a thing that I would change, 'cause you're a-maz -

VALERIE

Words and Music by SEAN PAYNE,
DAVID McCABE, ABIGAIL HARDING,
BOYAN CHOWDHURY and RUSSELL PRITCHARD

Up-beat Soul

Gm

-ter.

F

And I think of all the things ___ what you're do -

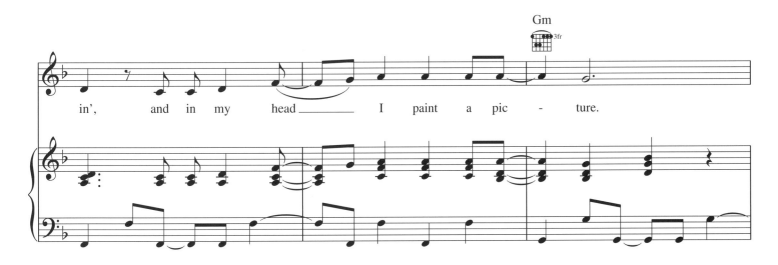

Gm

in', and in my head ___ I paint a pic - ture.

'Cause

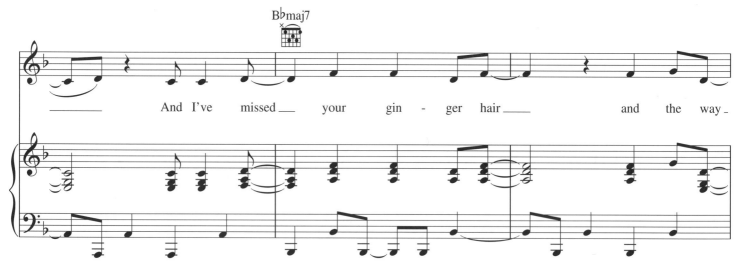

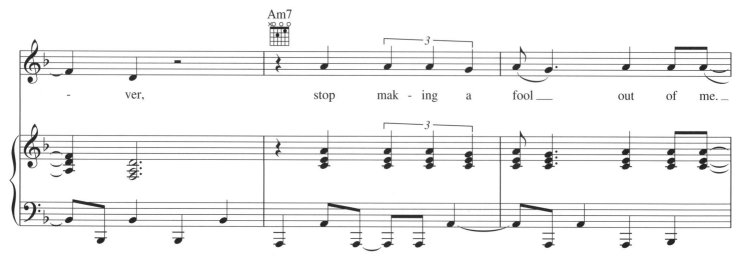

A - why don't you come on o -

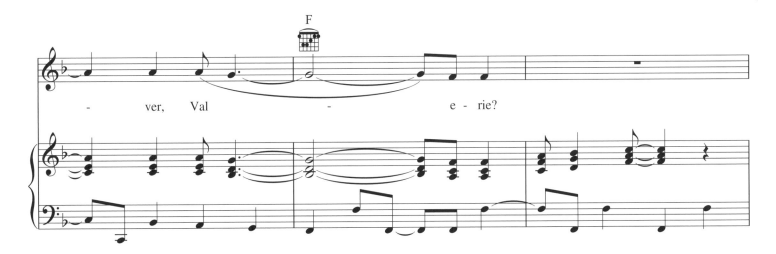

- ver, Val - e - rie?

Val - e - rie.

(Why don't you come on o - ver?) Val -

- e - rie.

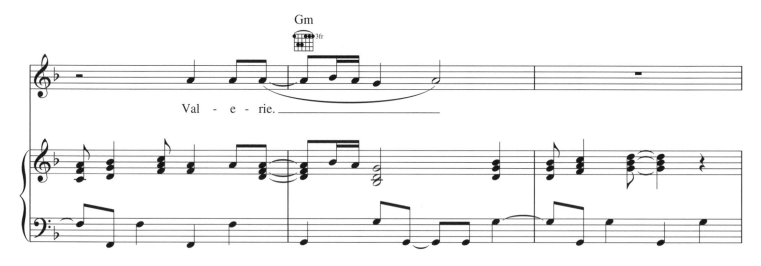

Val - e - rie. _____

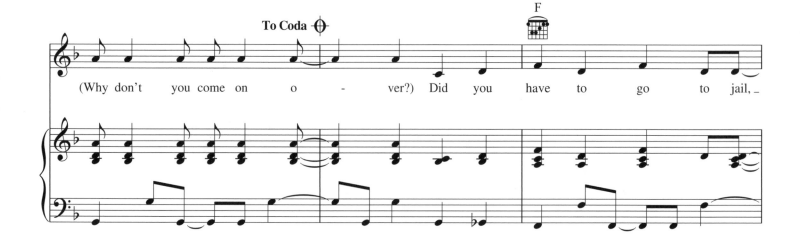

(Why don't you come on o - ver?) Did you have to go to jail,

___ put your house all up for sale? ___ Did you get a good

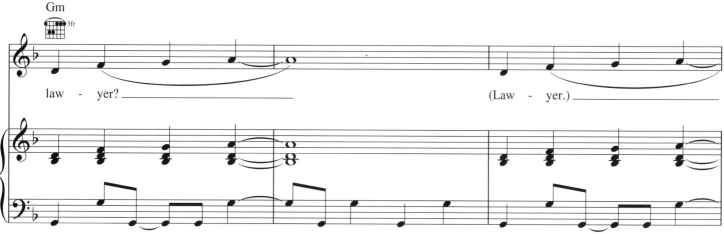

law - yer? _____ (Law - yer.) _____

_____ I hope you did - n't catch a tan, _____ I hope you'll

find the right man _____ who'll fix it for you. _____

_____ (Fix it for you?) _____ Now, are you

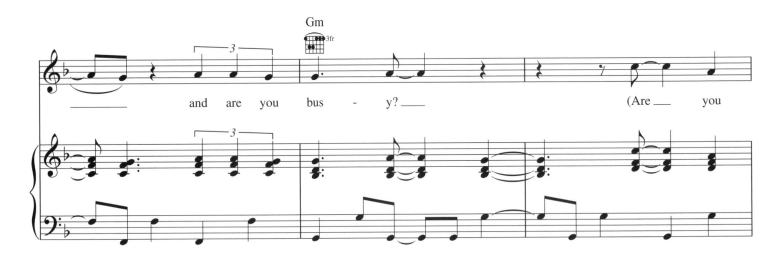

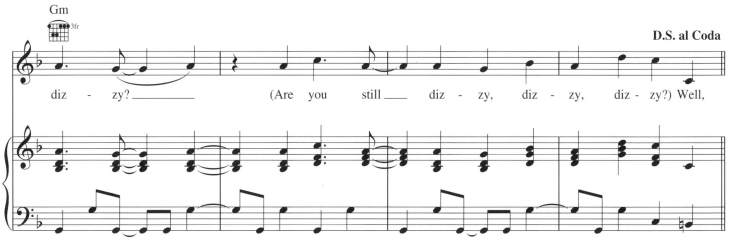

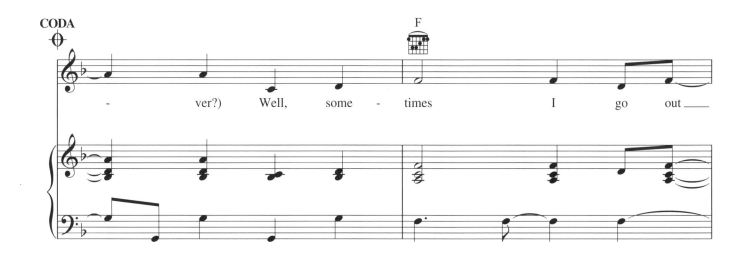

And I think of all the things ___ what you're do-

in', and in my head ___ I paint a pic - ture.

'Cause

since I've come on home, ___ well, my bod - y's been a mess. ___

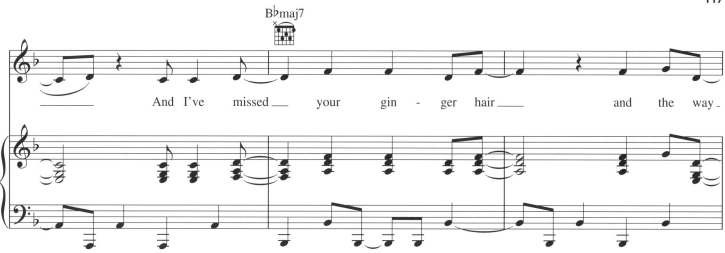

And I've missed ___ your gin - ger hair ___ and the way _

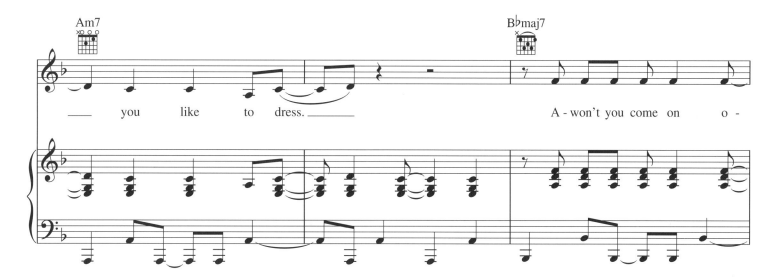

___ you like to dress. _____ A - won't you come on o -

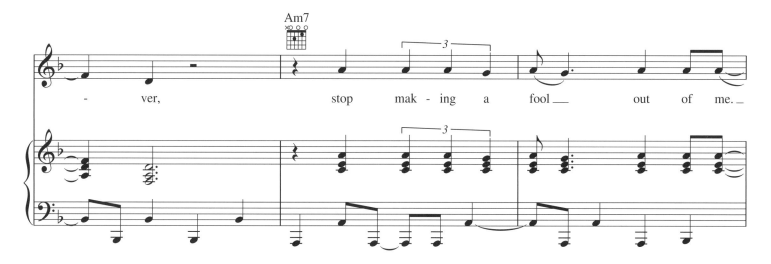

- ver, stop mak - ing a fool ___ out of me. _

A - why don't you come on o -

(I've Had)
THE TIME OF MY LIFE
from DIRTY DANCING

Words and Music by FRANKE PREVITE,
JOHN DeNICOLA and DONALD MARKOWITZ

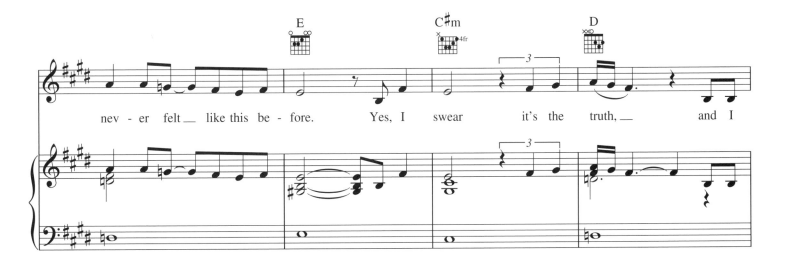

sy. _____

Both: Now with

pas - sion in our eyes _____ there's no way we could_ dis - guise _____ it se - cret -

ly. _____

So we

take each oth - er's hand _____ 'cause we seem to un - der - stand_ the ur - gen -

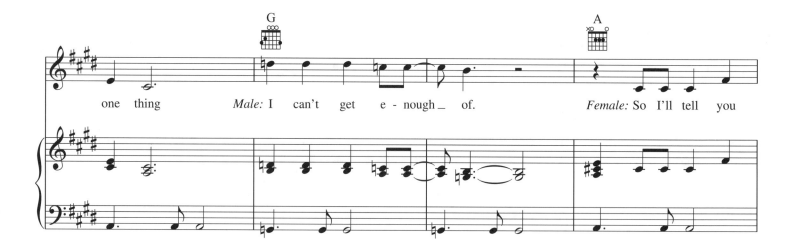

fore. Yes, I swear it's the truth, _____ and I owe it all to you. _____

Male: Hey, ba - by.

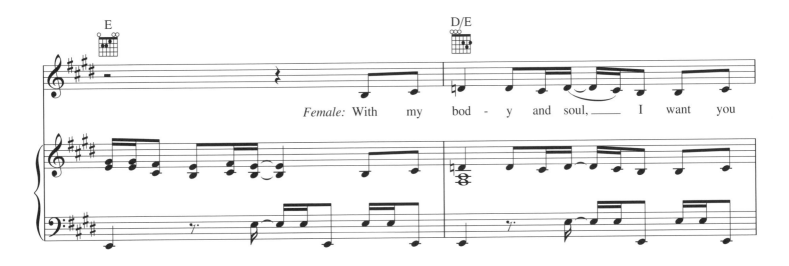

Female: With my bod - y and soul, _____ I want you

more than you'll ev - er know. _____ *Male:* So we'll

just let it go;___ don't be a - fraid to lose con - trol.___

Female: Yes, I know what's on ___ your mind when you say stay with me to-

night. ___ *Male:* Stay ___ with me. Just re - mem - ber, you're the

one thing ___ *Female:* I ___ can't get e - nough of. *Male:* So I'll tell you

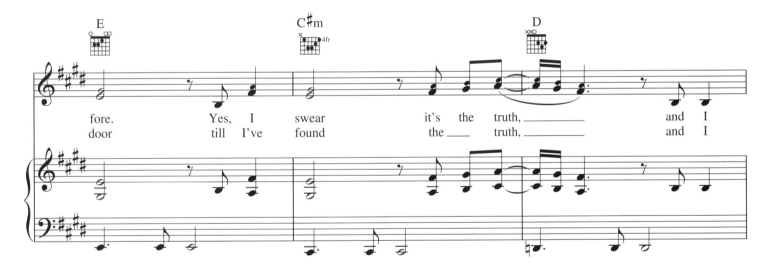

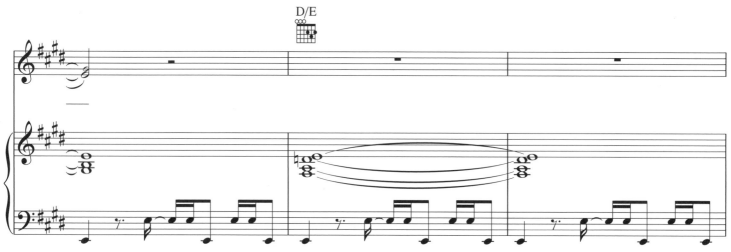

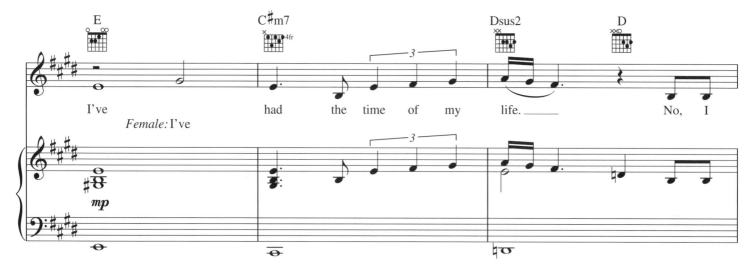

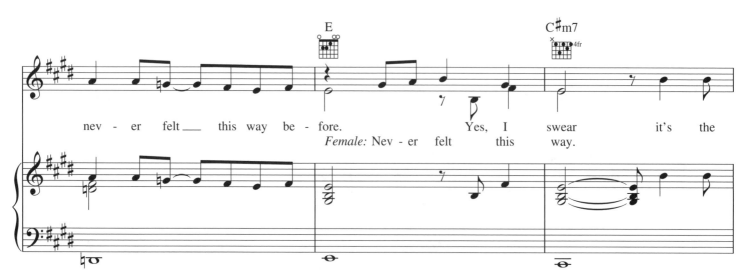

truth, ___ and I owe it all to you. ___ I've
I've

had the time of my life. ___ No, I nev - er felt ___ this way be -
had the time of my life. ___ And I've searched through ev - 'ry o - pen

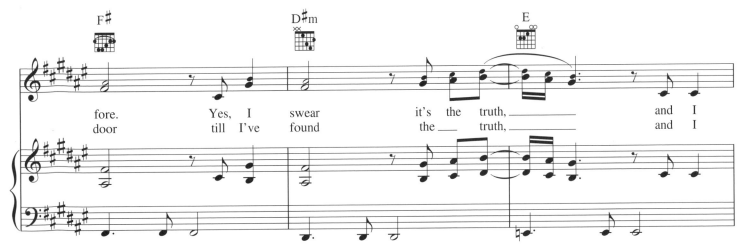

fore. Yes, I swear it's the truth, _____ and I
door till I've found the ___ truth, _____ and I

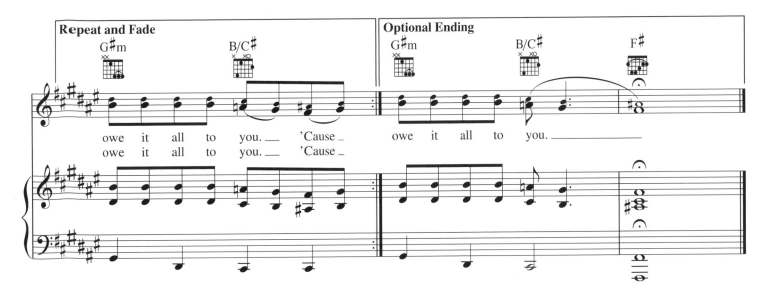

Repeat and Fade

owe it all to you. ___ 'Cause ___
owe it all to you. ___ 'Cause ___

Optional Ending

owe it all to you. _____